AMAVANT

AN UNKNOWN CIVILIZATION

notionpress
.com

AMAVANT
AN UNKNOWN CIVILIZATION

Akhilesh Chandra Upadhyay

notionpress.com

Notion Press

5 Muthu Kalathy Street, Triplicane,

Chennai - 600 005

First Published by Notion Press 2014

ISBN: 978-93-84391-56-0

Dedicated to my motherland.

PREFACE

Civilizations are never lost. They are eternal. All fundamental features of an ageing civilization get assimilated in the new world that follows its foot-steps. Thus, it is always there – alive – thriving in civilizations that it leaves behind. Everything is inter-connected – even Gods. 'Ahura-Mitra' of Zend Avesta, 'Mitra' of Vedic Aryans, 'Meher' or 'Mihir'of Persia and 'Mithrium' of Rome – all are one and the same. It is not difficult to observe the inter-connectedness of 'Uru-wa-na' (of Boghaz Koi inscription) with Greek 'Uranus' or Vedic 'Varuna'. Only physical aspects of civilizations change with time. Its huts, buildings or monuments might turn into ruins. Its villages or towns might get decimated. But its philosophies, beliefs and religious wisdom remain embedded, eternally, in all that lives afterwards. The building-bricks of any civilization are found, invariably, in the graveyards of preceding civilizations.

I am of firm opinion that twenty-first century will be remembered as the century of Indology. Be it the earliest hymns that were compiled by humanity, be it the invention of 'Zero' and decimal-system, be it the first solar calendar, be it the earliest urban-civilization of this earth – you can not overlook its eastern connection. Whether you get into the fundamentals of any religious philosophy or you study about any ancient civilization of this world – you will find that everything is inter-connected and, however dis-similar things might apparently be, you will find an under-current prevailing everywhere, which shall bear marks of its eastern connection. People from the east built Babylon. Indian 'Sal' and 'Sar' of Mesopotamia are no different. The time-span of 432000 years is one 'Kalyug' in India. In Mesopotamia, it is believed that this entire creation will be there – for exactly 432000 years. The Sun God of Egyptian Pharaohs – 'Ra' – is so closely related to the Sun God of the East – 'Ahu-Ra'. Days are not far off when we will find scholars from all over the world, engaged happily in pursuit of this new field of study – Indology.

Gods are inter-connected; civilizations are inter-connected; and so is humanity. It only needs a little conscious effort – to feel that affiliation and love. I am proud of all that was there in the past. I am proud of all values that I inherited. I am obliged to all those who created new philosophies in this world. My heart goes out to sincerely thank all Parsee (Zoroastrian) brothers and sisters. It was only because of them that I could trace this ancient civilization. Who else could provide me with hymns that are more than 5000 years old? I shall remain indebted to them – for ever. And before I put my pen down, I must thank Sheila, Arjun, Komal, Bhagyashree and Shuchi for their support. Only with their encouragement could I complete this book.

Gorakhpur, India. Akhilesh Chandra Upadhyay

Contents

INDO – IRANIANS

dUrAT haca ahmAT zaNtaoT[1]
dUrAT haca ai?Hat dai?haot

This is an Avestan hymn. It says – 'Far away is situated our towns, far away is situated our home land (country).' The Avesta speaking ancient Iranians knew that their roots were somewhere else. They knew that, long back, they had emigrated from a different land. It is all there in Avestan Gatha. These hymns of Gatha were compiled anytime before second millennium BC. Till then, memories of original home were not lost completely to the Aryans of ancient Iran. Its reminiscence can be found scattered, all over, in their earliest religious texts. But we failed to notice it and, as a result of which, we remained ignorant, for almost three thousand years, about this most significant mass-exodus of humanity.

In 1786, Sir William Jones discovered that there existed remarkable relationship between Sanskrit, Latin, Greek, German and Celtic languages. It was a discovery impregnate with significant consequences. The relationship clearly proved that all these European and Asian languages must have had a common origin. It was indicative of some common source of civilization, from which mankind had, in pre-historic times, branched off to all these countries of Asia and Europe. The underlying linguistic similarities proved that migrating Homosapiens of ancient period have had a distinct language of their own – from which had evolved all these modern languages. This primitive mother of all languages was called Proto-Indo- European language. It was believed that all these

1 Gatha – yasna – 57 – (para - 14).

languages had evolved from this hypothetical Proto-Indo-European (P-I-E) language. We call it hypothetical because, till date, it has not been attested in any form. It refers to very early days. Art of writing had not evolved. It must have been the dialect in which people used to communicate in those ancient days. However, there ensued a race to identify the original homeland of speakers of this mother of all languages. Different scholars came forward with different suggestions. Some said they were natives of the area that lies somewhere in the present day Austria-Hungary region. Some suggested that they could be original inhabitants of Arctic region or the region between Aral Sea and Afghanistan. There were many others who opined that they could have originated from the area adjoining the Caspian Sea. By late nineteenth century, it was accepted by general consensus that the original homeland of speakers of this Proto- Indo-European language was the steppes of Eurasia.

We are told that this area was inhabited by Proto-Indo-European (P-I-E) language speaking Aryans. It extended from Western Europe to, as far as China in the east. However, it is interesting to note that India was called 'Aryavart' during Vedic period. 'Aryavart' exactly means – the country of Aryans. Yet, Aryans were not considered to be the original inhabitants of India. Similarly, Iran literally means – 'the land of Aryans'. But it is believed that even Iran was not their original home. We are told that Aryans were a branch of Indo-European people who came into India and Iranian plateau in pre-historic times.

We are told that these Aryans of steppes lead a nomadic life. They were tribal people. In search of fresh pastures, they moved from one place to another. Their main occupation was cattle rearing. They were the ancestors of Indo-Iranian and Indo-Aryan speaking groups. During first half of second millennium BC they had reached southern parts of Central

Asia i.e. Bactria and Sogdia and North Western parts of Iran. But another branch of Indo-Europeans had fanned out further south and east. They entered Indian subcontinent a little later. They were the predeccessors of earliest Sanskrit speaking Indo-Aryans. But it was not an invasion of some no-man's land. On Indian soil, they encountered a well-settled agrarian community. The Northwestern terrain of India was, in those days, inhabited by the builders of Indus-Valley civilization. They were believed to be the natives of Indian soil. They were called Dravidians. It is believed that Dravidians were the pre-Vedic non-Sanskritic original inhabitants of India.

However, history seems to be the sum total of answers that leave behind questions twice in number. It often has more riddles than solutions. The idea of existence of some original homeland of ancestors of most of the known civilizations was derived from the basic linguistic affinity that was observed by Sir William Jones. But the exercise that began for determination of this original homeland was, from the very beginning, designed aimlessly. It generally followed the whimsical fantasies of scholars. The subject of quest referred to pre-historic times. It was impossible to get some readymade concrete and credible evidence. Therefore, people were free to select and adhere to the lead of their choice. Different theories were put forth about the original homeland of Aryans. Each theory emanated from accidental encounter with some kind of piece-meal bare fact. Each one of them had committed an error by not taking a wholistic view. Each one was misled. The linguistic and cultural similarities of diverse civilizations were sufficient to prove that all had evolved from a single ancient cradle. But no one ever tried to read through the pattern and contents of resemblances that were observable even through naked eyes. These elements of similarities were the traces of remote past. They present before us some of the significant aspects of P-I-E world. Their presence in different ethnic entities proves that our migrating ancestors carried them forward, wherever they went. They comprise of the conspicuous traits of ancient Aryan culture.

If we probe analytically into some of the common elements of ancient civilizations, we get a completely different picture of our ancestors. It almost changes our understanding of civilizations of pre-historic times. Let us take the example of ancient Indian and Iranian civilizations. India and Iran were neighboring countries. Each has had a rich and distinct culture of its own. Each was built by tribes that branched off from same stalk. Both inherited similar ideas that got assimilated in their linguistic, mythological and cultural fabric.

History teaches us that this P-I-E-language was carried along with the migrating Aryans wherever they had gone. Avesta – the earliest known language of Iranians had developed from this PIE-language. It was the language in which the earliest religious hymns were compiled on Iranian soil. Gatha (Yasna), Vishparad, Vendidad, Yasht, Khordeh Avesta etc. are the religious books of Parsees (Zoroastrians) and Avestan hymns are preserved in these books. Avesta literally means – revealed wisdom. It is an obsolete language and some of its words are considered more archaic than even Vedic Sanskrit. Thus, the religious books of Zoroastrians i.e. Parsees, which is written in Avestan language, becomes, beyond doubt, one of the first written records of mankind. The texts were compiled much before they could be reduced to writing. For centuries, they were passed on orally from generation to generation. They were reduced to writing only when phonetic alphabets were developed from Pahalavi script for inscribing the sounds of Avestan texts. Thus, the Avestan alphabet is far younger than the language it characterizes. Of all the sacred Parsee (Zoroastrian) literature Gatha is the oldest. It has 72 chapters, which are called 'Ha' or 'Haiti'. Ha 28 to Ha 53 are considered to be the earliest Avestan work. It is believed to be the creation of the Prophet Zoroaster himself.

Similarly, the Indo-Aryan branch of migrating Aryans had developed another language of their own. It was Vedic-Sanskrit and the earliest hymns that were compiled in Vedic Sanskrit are preserved in Rig-Veda, which is, again, considered to be the earliest religious book that came into existence on this earth. It comprises of ten 'Mandalas' and has 10552 Hymns. However, there are all together four Vedas. The remaining three are – Sam Veda, Yajur Veda and Atharv Veda. Like Avesta, even Vedas are believed to be the wisdom revealed by the Almighty. Could it be simple co-incidence? Why did it not strike to people that it was quite possible that this idea of divine revelation was existent in the so called P-I-E world and that migrating Aryans carried it along with them, wherever they went? It could have been a significant aspect of the mythology of so called P-I-E world. It is interesting to note that this idea was also incorporated in different other faiths of this world, that came into existence many centuries later. The earliest holy literatures of Judaism, Christianity and Mohammedan religion are also believed to be the revelations made directly by Almighty.

Vedic Sanskrit and Avesta are very closely related. Both these languages have striking similarities. Though a few of the Avestan words are more archaic but, by and large, each Avestan word has a corresponding similar word in Sanskrit. We observe noticeable changes between Vedic Sanskrit and the classical Sanskrit of later days. But hymns of Gatha i.e. Old Avestan texts are more allied to Vedic Sanskrit. The similarity is not restricted only to the use of exactly similar words. It can be distinctly noticed in the formation of hymns that are written in meters. Their feet and rhythm are strikingly similar.

Most probably, their ancient method of recitation was also exactly similar. Both these languages have like rules of grammar. Avesta and Vedic Sanskrit evolved in two different geographical locations independent of each other. It will be absurd to suppose that same words with similar meanings developed accidentally in two different civilizations. Rather, it can be fairly concluded that all such words, which are present in exactly identical form in both these languages, must have been the part of PIE – vocabulary. These words must have pre-existed the branching off of migrating Aryans. They were incorporated directly, without any transformation or modification in Avesta as well as in Vedic Sanskrit. Only then can their presence be justified in two different languages that developed independently in two different regions.

More than ninty percent of Avestan words have exactly identical corresponding words in Sanskrit. Similarly, the basic rules of grammar that are common in Avesta and Vedic Sanskrit must have also pre-existed the branching off of migrating Aryans. Thus, with vast resource of PIE- words and with the knowledge of basic grammar of PIE-language, we are in a position now, to frame sentences in the language that was spoken by early Aryans. In Gatha, we come across an Avestan line –

Masit&m dUrAT frasrUt&m[1]

'Masitam' is an Avestan as well as a Sanskrit word for 'water'. 'Durat' is again found in both languages. It refers to 'distance' and exactly stands for – 'from a distance'. Avestan 'frasrUt&m' is the corresponding identical of Sanskrit – 'prashrutam'. In both these languages, its meaning is - hearing. It is theSanskrit or Avestan word for 'hearing'. 'Masitam durat prashrutam' is both an Avestan as well as a Sanskrit expression that can be

1 Gatha – Yasna – 65 – (para - 3).

translated as – 'the sound of water is heard even from far distance'. We can reasonably conclude that all these words must had been the part of P-I-E vocabulary too, and that the migrating nomadic Aryans might have spoken the same line each time they heard the sound of falling or flowing water mass. Observe another Avestan line –

Kshatriya naam ahmi[1]

It can be translated as – 'Kshatriya is my name' or 'I am Kshatriya'. Each and every word of this line is present in Vedic Sanskrit as well – in exactly identical form and with exactly similar meaning. Even if this line was to be re-written in Sanskrit it will still remain the same. 'Kshatriya naam ahmi' is also the Sanskrit expression of 'Kshatriya is my name'. Therefore, we may presume that the so-called Aryans of Steppes would also have uttered the same – if they were to express similar thoughts. Each word must have existed in PIE – language as well. Similarly, 'Ayese Yesti' is an Avestan line. It is translated as – 'So it is'. This line is frequently appended to expressions that bear some kind of universal appeal in Gathic text. In Vedic Sanskrit also 'Ayese Yesti' means the same. We may, therefore, presume that this could have been one of the most frequently used lines in the original land of Aryans.

Let us analyze the word 'Arya' itself. It is improper to suggest that the branch of Indo-Europeans, that had reached Iran and India, was called – 'Aryan'. In fact the word 'Arya' is found identically in both Sanskrit and Avesta. This again proves that – 'Arya' itself, pre-existed in the P-I-E world, before the branching off took place. In their original land, these people must have called themselves – Aryans. After migration, when they settled down in two different countries, they continued addressing their community in the same fashion. It is also

1 Khordeh Avesta – Hormazd Yasht – (para – 15).

interesting to observe that words, along with its synonyms, are exactly identically present in Avesta, as well as, in Sanskrit. 'Hu wacha' and 'Uktha' are words which can be translated as 'good speech' or 'praise'. They are identically found in both languages with exactly similar meaning. Both these words must have been assimilated in Avesta and Sanskrit alike.

Avestan literature comprises of religious texts that reveal the philosophy of Zoroaster. 'Ahura' is the supreme God in Zoroastrian faith. It is generally believed that the name 'Ahura' was given by the Prophet Zoroaster himself, who founded the first monotheistic religion of this world. But the word 'Ahura' is identically found in Vedic literature as well. In Sanskrit, the word is 'Ahar' and it literally means 'day' or day-light'. It pertains to the Sun. The expression – 'Aharwe Mitra'- of Vedic literature is translated as 'Mitra, the morning Sun'. In Avestan texts also the word Ahura is used to convey either the Sun itself or the deity whose most significant physical manifestation is the Sun. 'Ahura – Mithra' of Avestan texts is exactly identical to 'Aharwe – Mitra' of Vedic texts. Thus, we may conclude that 'Ahura' was not a newly designed name of the Almighty in ancient Iran. Had it been so, then its presence would have been restricted to Avestan texts alone. The presence of corresponding identical word in Vedic literature as well, proves that even 'Ahura' or 'Ahar' must have pre-existed the branching off of Indo-Aryans and ancient Iranians. Even in the world of P-I-E speaking ancient Aryans, 'Ahura' or 'Ahar' must have been an attribute of the Sun.

But 'Kshatriya naam ahmi' is an important Avestan line. It conveys volumes about ancient Iranian social organization. Avestan or the Zoroastrian society was distinctly stratified into four-fold occupational class or caste system. These were Athornan, Ratheshtran or Kshatriya, Vastaryoshin and Hutokshan. The uppermost echelon comprised of 'Athornans'.

It was the priestly class of the society. 'Athornans' were people who conducted and supervised the worship of 'fire' and 'haoma' (soma). 'Ratheshtrans' literally means – 'charioteers' and it was the warrior class of the society. In later Avestan texts they are also called – 'Kshatriyas'. 'Vastaryoshins' were the traders and the tillers of soil where as 'Hutokshans' were artisans and labourers. This four-fold class or caste structure was, by and large, occupational in Avestan civilization.

We get similar set up even in Vedic India. Vedic society was also divided into four-fold exactly similar occupational class or caste structure. The upper most stratum in Vedic civilization too, consisted of the priestly class. It is surprising why an altogether new nomenclature was assigned to this class. The corresponding similar word for Avestan 'Athornan' was 'Atharvan' in Vedic Sanskrit. Even in Vedic society 'Atharvans' were people who used to conduct and supervise the worship of 'Fire' and 'Soma'. But the priestly class, as a whole, was called 'Brahman' in Vedic world. Similarly, the second caste or class in Vedic India also comprised of the warrior class. They were called – 'Kshatriyas'. The third in hierarchy were the 'Vaishyas'. 'Vastaryoshins' were called 'Vaishyas' in Vedic civilization. Like 'Vastaryoshins' of Avestan world, even 'Vaishyas' consisted of traders and farmers. 'Hutokshans' (Sutokshans) of Zoroastrian civilization had corresponding similar caste in Vedic world too. They were – 'Shudras'.

This unique and identical design of classification of members of society on a purely occupational basis could not have accidentally evolved in the two civilizations. Even caste or class names are also exactly similar. No other reason can be assigned to it. It will be absolutely rational to presume that the design was pre-existent and that it was assimilated into both civilizations without any change or modification. We have no other option but to believe that migrating Aryans carried the system of occupation-based stratification of society, wherever they went. Only then can its similarity be explained. Only then can the similar nomenclature of different occupational classes be explained.The four-fold caste structure pre-existed the mass exodus of Aryans from their original home. It further suggests that the Aryans were already divided into four distinct occupational classes before they could set foot on Iranian soil. Does it not contradict some of our long cherished irrational assumptions about the progress of civilization of our land? Even before mass exodus, Aryans have had complete package of four-fold occupational class system. The unique class or caste system, into which Vedic society was organized, was not the result of any encounter between Aryans and non-Aryans. The four-fold caste or class structure pre-existed the great migration. The 'Shudras' or 'Hutokshans' were not non-Aryans. They did not constitute any non-Aryan race. They were an essential component of Aryan society. They were Aryans themselves.

On the basis of above facts we can also conclude that the migrating Aryans were not nomadic people. A nomadic society does not contain specialized occupational groups. There is no requirement for it. People live merely by hunting or gathering eatables from nature. 'Hunter-gatherers' were people always on the move. They were not static. Members of any nomadic society work collectively for survival. They do not have people performing specialized functions within themselves. We may presume that rudimentary stage of trade and farming might be present in a given nomadic society but it cannot justify the existence of clearly defined four-fold caste or class structure. The development of occupational class or caste structure necessitates a large static social set-up where different kinds of work were expected of different groups from within. It was a design to ensure smooth functioning of complex static social organization. Migrating Aryans could not be nomadic people. They had distinct class of people engaged in different occupation. And most importantly, they had 'Vaishyas' who looked after trade and commerce. A nomadic society rarely has any concept of trade. But they had a distinct caste for traders. It proves that a large section of people were engaged in this profession of trade and commerce. Migrating Aryans were certainly not nomadic. They must have had a permanent settlement, which was not only agro-based but also had well developed trade and commerce.

But more significant fact is the similar style of compilation of hymns. Vedic and Avestan hymns came into existence in two different civilizations – independent of each other. Any similarity observed in the pattern of compilation of these sacred hymns must again be attributed to common origin. Identical style of compiling the feet and rhythm that is conspicuous in earliest Avestan and Vedic hymns, suggests that the art and its rules must have existed in the world of P-I-E speaking Aryans. Aryans of P-I-E world must have been compiling hymns in their original country. These rules of composition of hymns must have been carried along by the migrating Aryans to both Avestan and Vedic world alike. It also suggests that these migrating Aryans must have had a large number of sacred hymns of their own and that they must have come to their new homes with many such P-I-E Hymns. The art of writing had not evolved till then. Each hymn was committed to memory and passed on to succeeding generations. Therefore migrating Aryans must have come to new worlds with memories full of P-I-E hymns.

The art of compilation of hymns must have continued in their newfound homes. In Iran, it resulted in Zoroastrian hymns and in India it comprised of Rig-Vedic hymns. Even these newly composed hymns were preserved in the memories and passed on to succeeding generations. Art of writing came much later. Could it not be possible that some of the hymns of the Rig-Veda could actually be the part of earlier so called P-I-E hymns? Or that some of the Avestan hymns found in the Gatha could have been composed even before Aryans had set foot on Iranian soil? But there is no way to identify them. We have no means to pinpoint such hymns. They could be identified only on the basis of geographical clues that they might contain. If any of the Vedic hymns could narrate some geographical feature that could be specifically identified on ground anywhere beyond Indian subcontinent then we could have easily solved the mystery of so called P-I-E world. The question about the original home of Aryans could have been settled once and for all. But Avestan or Vedic hymns do not refer to any geographical feature beyond Afghanistan. This is strange though. To presume that all earlier hymns compiled in the so called P-I-E world were filtered out from the memory is something preposterous. It would have been a sacrilegious act even in those days. All religious hymns must have existed in the memories of migrating Aryans as sacred texts. Its inclusion in Avestan and Vedic religious texts was inevitable. But do we have even a single hymn that is identically found in liturgical texts of both religions? Yes. I think so. Twashtra was the engineer of Vedic divinities. 'Vajra' – the thunder like weapon of Lord Indra was designed by him. The name 'Twashtra' has been mentioned sixty-five times in Rig-Veda. Observe the following line of Vedic texts –

Takshantvashta vajram puruhoot dyumantam[1]

This line of Rig Veda can be translated as – 'the engineer Twashtra (Taksha) designed Vajra (thunder) which shines brilliantly'. 'Taksha' is a Sanskrit word that stands for –

1 Rig Veda – V – Sukta – 31 – (3873).

carpenter or engineer and is also used as the other name of Twashtra. Now compare this line with the following passage of Avestan texts –

Taxmvm dAmOiS upamanvm yazatvm yazamaide[1]

Each and every word of the aforesaid line is identically present in Vedic Sanskrit as well. In Sanskrit, the meaning of each word is as follows –

Taxmvm	–	engineer or carpenter or Twashtra himself
dAmOiS	–	thunder
upamanvm	–	to compare or to find similarity
yazatvm	–	to prepare or design
yazamaide	–	we worship hereby

Therefore, the whole line can be translated in Sanskrit as – 'we, hereby, worship Taksh, who engineered this thunder like thing'. I am of the opinion that it carries the same meaning even in Avesta as well. In both religious texts, the hymns refer to the invention of – Vajra. The hymns of Veda are no different from the hymns of Avestan Gatha. Both hymns attribute the invention of Vajra to Twashtra i.e. Taksh. The similarity can only be justified on grounds of common origin. This must have been one of those hymns that were compiled in the so called P-I-E world. It got incorporated identically in Zoroastrian as well as, in Vedic texts. And it gives out, fairly, the location of so called P-I-E world. The world of 'Twashtra' was the original home of Aryans. But the theory of Aryan invasion from steppes of Eurasia is accepted almost universally.

However, if we sincerely believe in it then we reach a stage where, especially in Indian-Iranian context, it becomes self-

---

1 Gatha – Yasna – 71 – para – (23).

contradictory. It is believed that nomadic Indo-Europeans reached India any time between 2000 BC and 1500 BC. They fought with the natives of this place, who were non-Aryans, and drove them down south. These Indo-Europeans or Aryans came in herds and occupied the Northern plains of India. For quite sometime they continued their nomadic style of living. Basically, they were hunter-gatherers who used to move about in search of fresh pastures. However, their way of living changed with the knowledge of agriculture. Once they took to agriculture, they started leading sedentary life and gradually, the first permanent settlements of ancient Aryans came into existence. Thus came into existence the earliest villages of Vedic Aryans. It was called – 'Vish'. It must have taken centuries to reach this stage. Hundreds of years must have elapsed in between the coming of Aryans and evolution of Aryan villages. It could have taken another few centuries when the population of some densely situated villages might have swelled to fill the inter-village gap to bring into existence a larger social unit - town. It was called 'Jana' in Vedic world.

But Avestan people and Vedic Aryans had parted at a very early stage. At that time – they were hunter-gatherers. They did not have concept of villages and towns. They had a common heritage that was reflected in their linguistic and mythological similarities, but their further developments were neither synchronized nor inter-dependent. They were free to design their further course of civilization. We do not know when the first village came into existence in Avestan world. But we know that even the Iranians called it – 'Vish'. We do not know when the first Iranian towns came into existence. But we know that, even in Avestan world, it was called – 'Jana' (Zan). Observe the following lines of Khordeh Avesta –

NmAnhe nmAno-paitim ashavanem ashahe ratum yazamaide[1]
Viso Vis-paitim ashavanem ashahe ratum yazamaide
Zanteush zantu-paitim ashavanem ashahe ratum yazamaide

The religious text gives out its meaning as – 'we revere the righteous master of the house, we revere the righteous master of the village, we revere the righteous master of the town'. 'Vis-paitim' of Avestan texts is exactly identical to 'Vish-pati' of Vedic civilization. 'Vish-pati' was the leader or master of the Vedic village. Similarly, the corresponding identical word for 'zantu-paitim' is 'jana-pati' in Sanskrit – that stands for 'the master of the town'.

Isn't that strange? According to the theory of Aryan invasion migrating Indo-Europeans were nomadic tribal. They did not lead a sedentary life. Therefore, they could not have any concept of Villages. Towns came even later. The terminology for villages and towns could not have evolved in so called P-I-E language. Villages and towns were non-existent in their world. Yet we have exactly identical terms for villages and towns in both Avestan as well as in Vedic culture. It could not be so without reason. We have no choice but to believe that even 'Vish' and 'Jana' was also derived from common roots. What else can justify this identical nomenclature of villages and towns? These terms must have pre-existed in so called P-I-E world. Does it not indicate that migrating Aryans were much more developed? That they were not tribal and nomadic? That they have had villages and towns in their original homeland? That the concept of 'Vish' and 'Jana' was brought by them alike in both Avestan and Vedic world? But the history of steppes of Eurasia presents an entirely different picture. It does not corroborate these facts. People in steppes lead a nomadic life even till the beginning of first millennium BC. Therefore, we have no other option but to conclude that

1 Khordeh Avesta – Aiwisruthrem Geh – para – (7).

the original homeland of Aryans could not be the steppes of Eurasia.

The mythological similarities of Avestan and Vedic culture clearly indicate the common inheritance of both civilizations. Indo-Iranians and Vedic people had many common deities. Mitra, Twashtra, Apam-Napatam, Usha, Vishwedeva and Aryaman are some of the divinities found both in Avestan as well as in Vedic culture. The Goddess Fire was one of the most important divinities in both civilizations. She was called 'Athro' in Avestan world and Vedic people called her – 'Agni'. The importance given to the Goddess Fire was so much that the first Hymn of Rig-Veda is devoted to her. Also, Zoroastrians are believed to be fire-worshipping people. Similarly, 'Soma' of Rig-Veda is described as 'Haoma' in Avestan texts. In many Avestan words we observe that Sanskrit 'S' is substitued by 'H'. Avestan Haoma (Vedic Soma) was a plant from which some kind of elixir or exhilarating drink was obtained. This drink was offered in almost all religious ceremonies to appease the divinities. It had invigorating effect and was often used by people before going to war. The similar process, that was employed to extract this juice, is described in detail in both Avestan and Vedic texts. The twigs of Haoma plant were crushed in a stone mortar and the juice thus obtained was strained through a sieve. It was then mixed with water or milk and sprinkled in the holy fire during the religious ceremony – 'Havana' - so that it could reach Gods. Fire was considered as the most powerful purifying agent that could remove all impurities and yet, could never be contaminated by anything. What else could be more suitable vehicle for carrying worldly things to divinities? In 'Haoma Yasht'of Avestan texts this Haoma is, at places, depicted as an important Zoroastrian deity who gave Haoma juice to the mankind. The description of Soma of Vedic texts is exactly similar too. Even in Vedic texts we get – 'Somadeva', who presides over the Soma plant and its juice. In Rig-Veda, maximum number of Hymns is dedicated to Indra (the God of thunder and rain), Agni (the God of fire) and Soma. The entire ninth Mandala of Rig-Veda is devoted to Soma. 'Indra' – the Vedic God of thunder – was considered to be very fond of Soma-elixir. Both Vedic and Avestan texts give exactly similar account of extraction and filtration of elixir from the twigs of Soma plant. In both civilizations Soma or Haoma was also considered to be the deity who looked after the plant and its elixir.

These mythological similarities could not have evolved accidentally. Once again we will have to attribute these developments to the theory of common origin. We ought to presume that all these divinities must have been pre-existing in religious beliefs of the so called P-I-E language speaking Aryans. We will have to admit that migrating Indo-Europeans or Aryans were people possessing rich mythological background that got manifested alike in Zoroastrianism as well as in Vedic religion. They came to their new world with a distinct so called P-I-E religion. They already had a mature faith - before they left their original home. Today's Hinduism and Zoroastrian religion contain many important elements of their religious beliefs. The world of Twashtra, Usha, Mitra, Apam Napatam, Vishwedeva, Aryaman and Soma (Haoma) was the original home land of so called P-I-E speaking ancient Aryans.

However, Soma or Haoma reveals an interesting story. The identical name of this elixir-producing twig suggests that the name Soma or Haoma was also pre-existing and that the migrating Aryans were aware of this plant. The similar method of extraction of elixir and its identical use in religious ceremonies must have been the continuation of old practices that was prevalent in the so called P-I-E world. Thus we may conclude that the mountain-peak, on which Soma plant was found, must have been an important geographical feature of the so called P-I-E world. Since the use of Soma was an integral part of their religious activities, its requirement must have been of immense importance. It was a 'Holy' drink. It was the most sacred thing that existed on this earth. Its continuous supply was essential in day-to-day activities of ancient Aryans. We may therefore, presume that the migrating Aryans must have organized or evolved some means for its regular procurement. It was a rare plant and could not be available all along their way. The only way to ensure its regular supply was to evolve the practice of fetching it from their homeland. In every band or group of migrating Aryans there might have existed some kind of team that continued to go back to the original land to fetch these Haoma-twigs. Haoma-factor must have been the umbilical cord that kept migrating Aryans inseparable from their original home. Fetching Haoma twigs must have been a very important aspect. Its mention was inevitable. Avestan and Vedic texts give vivid account of extraction and filtration of Haoma juice. Yet, they are silent about its method of procurement. They do not mention about any journey back to their original home that was required to obtain the religious Haoma plant. It is strange though. And what happened once they settled in their newfound homes? Did they get Haoma twigs in Iran as well as in India? Was it available in both these places simultaneously? If not, then they had no other option but to continue the process that they might have adopted all along their way. But Vedic and Avestan religious texts are silent about it. Rather, both texts describe that it was found on top of a particular mountain. Could it be that we have gone wrong somewhere? I think so. In all probability, Avesta speaking ancient Aryans and Aryans of Vedic civilization never left the country of Soma.

Who were, then, the common ancestors of Avestan Iranians and Vedic Aryans? It is evident that our ancestors belonged to a civilization that was much more evolved than what is generally believed. They have had an urban or semi-urban civilization in their original homeland. They came from the land of 'Vish' and 'Jana'. But surprisingly, all these factors have been overlooked till date. One wonders why they were considered nomadic or barbaric. Could it be because this distinctly evolved state of affairs did not fit in well with the theory of Aryan invasion? To admit that migrating Aryans had originated from the civilized world of 'Vish' and 'Jana' would negate the proposition of European origin. However, let us now, identify a few of our common ancestors. Observe the following lines of Avestan Gatha –

WIwaMhI m&m paoiryO maKy0[1]
astwaiqyAi hunUta gaEthyAi
hA ahmAi aCiS vrvnAawi
taT ahmAi jasaT Ayaptvm
Yat he puqro us zayata
Yo Yimo xCaEtO hw&qBO

This hymn of 'Haoma Yasht' narrates the words of Haoma. Zoroaster had inquired from Haoma about the person who had first pressed Haoma twigs. In Zoroastrian religious texts the hymn is translated as –

'Vivanhvat (was) the first mortal (who) pounded me in the material world, Unto him this blessing was granted, unto him this profit was accrued; namely, to him a son was born------ He was blessed with a son called Yima the king. This is what Haoma told Zoroaster[2].'

---

1 Gatha – Yasna – 9 – para – (4).

2 Avesta Reader – Text Translation by Ervad Prof. M.F. Kanga – (Haoma Yast - page 9-10).

Interestingly, we have identical characters in Vedic texts as well. Avestan 'Vivanhvat' can be written as 'Vivanswat' in Sanskrit because 's' is found invariably substituted by 'h' in Avestan language. Also, the presence of - 'n' in 'Vivanhwat' is the characteristic feature of Avestan rules that produced colloquial variants. In Avestan texts, we often find references where Avestan 'Ahu' becomes 'Anhu' and 'Vohu' becomes 'Vanhu'. Thus the main word must have been simply – Vivaswat. Isn't that surprising? Vedic 'Vivaswat' was one of the most important sages of ancient Indian mythology. At places, this Vivaswat is also mentioned as Vivaswan in Vedic texts. In para – 5 of Yasna – 9, we again get clear mention of the fact that Yima was the son of Vivanhwat.

The hymn says –

Yimo WIwaMuhato puqrO[1]

Now observe the following lines of Sam Veda –

When prayers impel the golden hued Haoma[2]
To hasten from Vivaswan's place

Vedic 'Vivaswat' was one of the most important sages. This hymn of Sam Veda describes that he was credited with preparation of Haoma (Soma) juice. Is it any different from the facts described in Avestan texts? Even Vedic texts describe that Vivaswat was blessed with a son called 'Yam Vaivaswat'. 'Yam Vaivaswat' was called so because he was the son of 'Vivaswat'. Those days it was a common practice in India and learned men and sages carried their family names along with their own names – to preserve the identity of their paternal lineage. Thus, 'Daman Yamayan' was called so because he was the son of 'Yama'. Vedic sage 'Sumitra Kaots' was called so because his father's name was 'Kuts'. This Vedic 'Yam

1 Gatha – Yasna – 9 para – (5).

2 Sam Veda – Part – 2 - Book – VIII – Chapter – I – (VI).

Vaivaswat' is mentioned at fifty different occasions in the Rig-Veda. His mother was – 'Saranyu'. Avestan texts consider 'Yima' as the first human being who died and hence, after his death, he became the God of the Dead. Even Vedic Hymns describe 'Yam Vaivaswat' as the Lord of the Dead, who looks after all the deceased human beings. Things are precisely clear. Avestan texts and Vedic literature have been referring to the same ancestors. Vedic mythology says that Yama had a sister. Her name was 'Yami'.They were twins. In Persian mythology too, they are present as Yima and Yimaka.

Similarly, Gathic texts describe that 'Atwya' was the second mortal to pay homage to Haoma and to press Haoma twigs. He was blessed with a son named 'Trit' about whom it is said that he beheaded a three-headed demon. We get similar description in the eighth Hymn of tenth Mandala of Rig-Veda, where it is described that 'Trit Aptya' had borrowed weapons from his father to defeat and kill the three-headed demon. 'Trit' was the son of 'Aptya', that is why he was called – 'Trit Aptya'. There is another very interesting Avestan hymn about 'Trit', who is considered as the third mortal to have pressed Haoma twigs. Observe the following lines –

Trit, the most powerful of Sama family, was the third mortal[1] *who pounded me (Haoma) in this material world.*

Now, observe and compare it with the following lines of Sam Veda –

The place that is concealed has gained[2]
a share of Trita's pressing stones.

The hymn describes the pressing stones that were used by 'Trit' for making Haoma (Soma) juice.

1 Avesta Reader – Text Translation by Ervad Prof. M.F. Kanga – (Haoma Yast – page – 21).

2 Sam Veda – Part – 2 - Book – III – Chapter – II – (XVIII).

Things are clear. Both Avestan and Vedic texts have been referring to same persons. Vivaswat, Yam Vaivaswat, Aptya and Trit-Aptya must have been their common ancestors. They must have existed any time before Indo-Iranians and Vedic-Aryans got separated. They were the sages of the original home land. Their contributions were significant and they were remembered with equal reverence, even generations after, when the migrating Aryans branched off and settled in two different worlds. However, it is interesting to observe that, in Rig-Veda, we have many hymns that are claimed to have been given or compiled by Yam Vaivasvat and Trit- Aptya. The following hymn of Rig-Veda is attributed to Trit-Aptya.

Aham so asmi yah pura sute vadami kani chit[1]

It says – 'I was chanting the holy mantras (hymns) during the ritual of extraction of Soma.' In Rig-Veda too, Trit-Aptya has been credited with the supervision of ceremony of Soma worship. Rather, in Rig-Veda, he himself proclaims it through the aforesaid hymn. Similarly, the following hymn of Rig-Veda is attributed to Yam Vaivaswat. It says –

Vaivaswatam sangamanam jananam Yamam.....[2]

The hymn can be translated as – 'all human beings are destined to finally go to Yam, the son of Vaivaswat (because he is the one who looks after the deceased)'.

Could it be that these hymns of Trit-Aptya and Yam-Vaivaswat were compiled in the world of some Indo-Europeans, who spoke P-I-E language? Could it be that they are part of those sacred hymns that were compiled in the so called P-I-E world? Before Aryans embarked upon migration to countries like Iran and India? These mythological similarities of Zoroastrian Gatha and Rig-Veda can not be explained in

1 Rig Veda – 1 – Sukta - 105 – (1153).
2 RigVeda – 10 – Sukta – 14 – (8903).

any other way. It could not simply be a coincidence. Not only the names of our ancestors are similar, even their deeds and related stories are also identical. The only explanation to this similarity is again – the common origin. Prior to the migration of Aryans, these ancestors must have existed in the so called P-I-E world. That is the reason why they were remembered alike in both these civilizations. The hymns of Zoroastrian Gatha and Rig-Veda were compiled in two different geographical locations. But the names of these ancestors and their stories got incorporated alike in both these scriptures. Vedic and Avestan hymns attest the fact that Yam-Vaivaswat, Aptya and Trit-Aptya were sages who pre-existed the branching off of migrating Aryans. But where was this P-I-E world?

Vedic civilization flourished in and around Indus valley. In Vedas, this region was called – 'Sapt-Sindhu'. 'Sapt-Sindhu' stands for 'the seven rivers'. They comprised of river Indus and its tributeries. We often find Vedic hymns deifying the river Indus. These hymns, on their own, give out the exact location where Vedic Aryans lived. Could it be that Vaivaswat, Yam-Vaivaswat, Aptya and Trit-Aptya lived in the area around river Indus? But why don't Avestan hymns corroborate this truth? Although we get many references of 'Sapta-Sindhu' in Avestan hymns too, yet we do not get a single hymn that conveys, directly or indirectly, the fact that our common ancestors hailed from the region of Indus. The region of Sapta-Sindhu was so close to Iran. If this was their original home land; if this was the home land of their ancestors, then its mention was inevitable. But Avestan hymns do not accord much importance to river Indus. On the other hand, the most significant river of Avestan Gatha is 'Ardvi-Sur'. Could it be that Avestan civilization flourished on and around the banks of river Ardvi-Sur? Could it be that Avestan society was sustained by the waters of Ardvi-Sur and as such, this river was accorded maximum importance in Zoroastrian Gatha? And there is yet another possibility. The sages of ancient Iran, who compiled Avestan hymns, missed their land of origin. They knew that their home-land was situated far away. They missed their homes, villages and towns that were left behind. Could it be that river Ardvi Sur was the most important river of their original homeland? Let us find out more about it.

Ardvi Sur

YazAi Apvm arvdwIm sUr&m anAhit&m[1]

It says – 'salutations to undefiled waters of Ardvi Sur'. This Avestan hymn is dedicated to river Ardvi Sur. Ancient Zoroastrians worshipped this river. We find innumerable hymns attributed to river Ardvi Sur in Gatha, Khordeh Avesta and Vendidad. These are ancient holy texts of Zoroastrian religion. In Khordeh Avesta, a whole chapter is dedicated to river Ardvi Sur. It is called 'Ardvi Sur Niyaesh'. Ardvi Sur was the most sacred river of ancient Zoroastrians. But, as on date, the river remains shrouded with mystery. It is yet to be identified. Some scholars suggest it was a celestial river that originated from the mythical Mount Hukairiya. But there is another school of thought that considers Ardvi Sur as some terrestrial river of ancient Iran, which is yet to be identified on ground. The mystery of river Ardvi Sur is overwhelming. Its proper knowledge might contain volumes about ancient Aryan civilization. Pursuit of its truth is going to be an exercise of significant historical interest. Let us begin our quest through Avestan hymns. These hymns were compiled anytime before second millennium BC. They contain innumerable references about river Ardvi Sur. The earliest Avestan hymns are contained in Gatha. Observe the following line of Gatha –

zarayO WourukCvm YazamaidE[2]

'WourukCvm' is pronounced as – Vourukashvm. The hymn says – 'we revere, hereby, the river of Vourukash'. This hymn pertains to Ardvi Sur. Ardvi Sur, in Avestan hymns, was also called the 'river of Vourukash'. But interestingly, in Avesta-

1 Gatha – Yasna – 65 – para – (1).

2 Gatha – Yasna – 42 – para – (4).

English dictionary, Vourukash is explained as Caspian Sea. If it was so, then the river of Vourukash could not be a mythical river. It must have existed on ground. It had to be related to Caspian Sea. Ardvi Sur had to be terrestrial. Another Avestan hymn almost confirms it. Observe the following hymns -

masit&m dUrAT frasrUt&m[1]
YA asti awawaiti masO
Yatha WIspI imI ApO
YI zvamA paiti frataciNti

Each and every word of this Avestan hymn has exactly identical corresponding word in Sanskrit as well. In both languages they convey similar meanings. 'Masit&m dUrAT frasrUt&m', both in Avesta and Sanskrit, conveys the same meaning. It is – 'the waters can be heard from far distance'. Similarly, 'YA asti awawaiti masO' means 'which is a huge body of water masses'. 'Yatha WIspI imI ApO' can be translated as – 'where this water of the world' and 'YI zvamA paiti frataciNti' is – 'which falls on the ground (earth)'. The hymns describe river Ardvi Sur. It was a huge water mass that fell from a height. The sound of water-fall could be heard from far distance. This is certainly not the description of a celestial river. The waters of Ardvi Sur fell on earth producing thunderous sound that could be heard from far distance. There is no reason for any doubt. Ardvi Sur was definitely a terrestrial river.

Ancient civilizations flourished on riverbanks. The perennial source of water used to be the lifeline of ancient world. Rivers were the easiest means of irrigation and the earliest agriculture-based settlements were virtually dependent on mighty rivers that could supply enough water throughout year. Their regular floods nourished the fields and as such, they were considered the giver of life and fertility. The first Chinese

1 Gatha – Yasna – 65 – para – (3).

settlements were seen on the banks of Yellow River. Indus Valley civilization flourished along Indus and its tributaries. The trend was universal and without exception. Mesopotamia exactly means – 'between rivers'. It was the stretch of land between Tigris and Euphrates rivers. Here evolved one of the most important riverside civilizations where earliest urban societies came into existence. The ancient civilization of Egypt is attributed, genuinely, to river Nile. These river-centric cultures, in turn, deified rivers that proved to be the umbilical cord of their existence. In Greek mythology, Nilus was the son of Oceanus and Tethys. Nilus represented Nile and was considered the river God. In Egyptian mythology Anuket was the personification and Goddess of the river Nile. Her temple was erected at the Island of Seheil, where she became the Goddess of fertility. River Indus was worshipped in Vedic India and Aryans of Northern Gangatic plains of India deified river Ganges as Mother Goddess. Similarly, the most important river of Avesta speaking Zoroastrians was Ardvi Sur. The ancient Iranian civilization must have flourished on its banks. It is the most significant river of Avestan texts. Ardvi Sur is as holy a river to Zoroastrians as Ganges is to Hindus.

But can we identify Ardvi Sur with any of the existing rivers of Iran? There are very few rivers in Iran. Most of them are seasonal. Sepid Rud, Aras and Karun are the only rivers that flow round the year. Aras flows in the North West. It does not originate in Iran. Aras rises from the Bingol Duglas mountain of Turkey, where it is called – Aras Nehri. Hence, it cannot be Ardvi Sur. Ancient Iranians were familiar with the place of origin of Ardvi Sur. They could hear the sound of waterfall as the river descended on ground. It could not be in Turkey. It had to be in near vicinity. Aras cannot be identified with Ardvi Sur. Sefid Rud flows in the North. Literally, Sefid Rud is 'white river'. It is the second largest river of Iran.

Sefid Rud originates from Kurdish Mountains and falls into Caspian Sea. But Sefid Rud could not be the river Ardvi Sur. In antiquity, this river was known as Mardus. There is yet another reason for not considering these two rivers as Ardvi Sur. They flow in the North. They do not flow through central regions of Iran. But Avestan Gatha describes Ardvi Sur as follows –

A WispO maiDyO Yaozaiti[1]

The hymn describes the location of river Ardvi Sur. 'WispO' is corresponding identical of Sanskrit word – 'wishvo'. It stands for – world. Avestan 'maiDyO' is – centre or middle. The corresponding identical of 'maiDyO' in Sanskrit is – 'madhyo'. Avestan 'Yaozaiti'or 'Yojati' of Sanskrit can be translated here as – to mark, to unite. The Hymn describes that river Ardvi Sur marks or flows through the central regions of this world. Sefid Rud and Aras do not flow through central parts of Iran which was the world of Zoroastrians. Therefore, neither could be identified as river Ardvi Sur. Karun is the largest river of Iran. In Biblical accounts its name is Pishon or Pastigris. Even Karun cannot be identified with Ardvi Sur because it originates in Zurd Kuh Mountain and falls into Persian Gulf. It does not fall into Caspian Sea. Therefore, it cannot be the river of Vourukash. The river of Vourukash had to be related to Caspian Sea. Thus, we are back to square one. Ardvi Sur cannot be identified with any of the existing rivers of Iran. Should we look beyond? There is an important line in Avestan Gatha.

Yo hiStaitE maidim zrayaMhO WourukaCahe[2]
ZarayO wourukaCvm YazamaidE

Let us analyze the meaning of each word of this hymn. 'WourukaC' i.e. 'Vourukash' is the only word which is not

1 Gatha - Yasna – 65 – para – (4).
2 Gatha – Yasna – 42 – para – (4).

found in Vedic Sanskrit. All remaining Avestan words have their corresponding identical word in Sanskrit as well. 'Yo' is both Avestan and Sanskrit word for – 'where' or 'which'. 'hiStaitE' is an Avestan word that expresses the meaning – 'to exist'. It is derived from the root – 'Sta'. It is identically found in Sanskrit as well. The root word of 'zrayaMhO' is 'zraya'. In both languages, it is translated as – 'river'. 'maidim' is 'earth', 'land' or 'ground'. In Sanskrit the word 'medini' means 'earth'. 'YazamaidE' is the corresponding identical of 'Yazam ide' of Sanskrit language. In both languages, its meaning is – 'we worship hereby'. Thus, the whole passage can be translated as –

> 'The river, which exists on the grounds of Vourukash,
> We worship, hereby, that river of Vourukash.

Strictly according to this Avestan hymn Vourukash is the name of place and Ardvi Sur flows through Vourukash. It contradicts the meaning proposed by Avesta-English dictionary. Vourukash could not be Caspian Sea. On its ground flowed the most important river of Zoroastrian Gatha. Therefore, let us begin our probe all over again. We have three important clues. Firstly, Ardvi Sur was a terrestrial river. Secondly, it flowed through central regions of Zoroastrian world. Thirdly, Ardvi Sur flowed through Vourukash and hence, it was also called the river of Vourukash. But the river must have flowed across many different places. However, it was named after Vourukash alone. Therefore we may conclude that Vourukash must have been, in those ancient days, a significantly famous place. There is an important information about this place in 'Yasna Haptanghaiti' of Zoroastrian Gatha It says –

And we sacrifice to that sea of Vourukash[1]

1 Avesta: Yasna – Sacred liturgy and Gatha/Hymns of Zarathushtra –Yasna Haptanghaiti – 42 - translated by L H Mills (from the Sacred Books of the East).

Now, we may fairly presume that Vourukash was a famous place situated on some sea-shore and that even the sea itself was referred to as the sea of Vourukash in those ancient days. Ardvi Sur must have flowed across Vourukash and fell into the sea of Vourukash. But is there any such place in Iran that can be identified with Vourukash? If we look through the coastal regions of Caspian Sea and Persian Gulf, we do not find any place that bears even the slightest relation with the name Vourukash. On the other hand, we have a place in India that bears absolute resemblance with the name Vourukash. It is situated on sea-shore and has a mighty river too, flowing across. It is 'Varukaksha'. Varukaksha was the ancient name of Bharooch. We find its mention in ancient Pali scriptures. Modern Bharooch is situated on the banks of Arabian Sea. Also, Narmada - the mightiest river of Deccan Plateau – flows through Bharooch. And surprisingly, Narmada flows exactly through central regions of India. But how can we identify river of Vourukash of Zoroastrian Gatha with a river like Narmada? Besides, Avesta was the language of ancient Iranians. It became extinct even before first millennium BC. The hymns of Gatha were compiled in Avesta. The river of Vourukash has to be in Iran.

But Varukaksha bears absolute resemblance with the name Vourukash. Therefore, first of all, let us relook into any possible connection between the rivers Narmada and Ardvi Sur. 'Sur' literally means 'river'. Thus, we may presume that the name of the river of Vourukash must have been 'Ardvi'. Now, Ardvi and Narmada have become somewhat closer. There exists an apparent similarity between the two names. Water and water-bodies were worshiped in Avestan society. 'Namo Ardvebhyo' is both Avestan as well as a Sanskrit expression. In both languages, it means – 'salutations to Ardvi'. If you chant aloud 'Namo Ardvebhyo' repeatedly, observe how easily it tends to become 'Narmadebhyo'. Could it be that, in antiquity, Narmada was called Ardvi? And that Narmada is the abbreviated form of 'Namo Ardvebhyo'? We cannot say much about it and there is no way to proceed further. In this regards, only Avestan hymns can be of any help.

The hymn that is repeated maximum number of times in all Avestan religious texts is – 'raEwatO XarvanaMuhatO'. In Avestan translations, the word 'raEwatO', when applied to human beings, is considered to mean 'rich' or 'wealthy'. But if it refers to divine beings, then it is considered to stand for 'brilliant', 'splendid' or 'radiant'. Similarly, 'XarvanaMuhatO' is translated as – 'possessed of glory'. Thus, in Avestan religious books, 'raEwatO XarvanaMuhatO' is explained as – 'radiant and possessed of glory'. They believe that the hymn is attributed to Lord Ahura. In Zoroastrian scriptures we often come across the following hymn –

ahurahe mazdI raEwatO XarvanaMuhatO[1]

In Avestan religious books it is translated as – 'Lord Ahur Mazda, the radiant and possessed of glory'. But this can not be the true explanation of the said hymn. This hymn ought to have some other meaning. Let us look at another place where this hymn is given somewhat differently.

daquCo ahurahe mazdI raEwatO XrvnaMuhatO[2]

In this hymn 'daquCo' (dathusho) is the only extra word that has been added. In Avestan texts it is translated as an act of giving. The root word here is – 'Da', which is identically found in Sanskrit as well. 'daquCo' stands for – gave or to give. But nobody gave to us Lord Ahura Mazda, the radiant and possessed of glory. Rather, Lord Ahura is himself the ultimate source of this entire creation. According to Zoroastrian

1 Gatha – Yasna – 24 – para – (28).
2 Gatha – Yasna – 16 – para – (3).

mythology nothing pre-existed God Ahura. How do we explain the meaning of 'daquCo' here? 'Lord Ahur Mazda, radiant and possessed of glory' is a complete sentence. It does not grant space for any act of giving. Therefore, it will be worthwhile to analyze afresh the meaning of 'raEwatO XarvanaMuhatO' of Avestan texts.

We observe that, throughout religious scriptures, different kinds of phonetic transcriptions have been accorded to the word – 'XarvanaMuhatO'. At different places, it is written somewhat differently. In Khordeh Avesta (Hoshbam) it is mentioned as – 'kharenanguhato'. At other places, it is also mentioned as – 'xarenanuhaite', 'Kharenanguhastemem' or 'Hvarenanguhastemem'. It shows how difficult it must have been to phonetically inscribe the texts of Avesta in Sassanian-Pahlavi script. The texts were compiled much before they could be reduced to writing. Art of writing had not evolved till then. For centuries, the hymns were passed on orally, from generation to generation. They were reduced to writing only when phonetic alphabets were developed from Pahalavi script for inscribing the sounds of Avestan texts. The language of the text and the script were mismatched. Avesta had become extinct long before. Even in those days, its words were not properly understood. This must have been the reason for phonetically inscribing Avestan texts. And once they were reduced to writing, the practice of memorizing and passing it on, orally, to succeeding generations was given up. As a result, today we are in possession of fragments of only the phonetic inscriptions with all their inherent limitations.

However, let us come back to re-look into the meaning of 'raEwatO XarvanaMuhatO'. It is interesting to note that, at places, 'raEwatO' is also used as a proper noun in Zoroastrian world. That is when it conveys the name of a mountain. It is considered to be the name of a mountain in 'Khorasan', where 'Atar-Burzin' – the 'Holy-Fire' is established. But isn't that strange? Even Indian mythology is full of references of a mountain – 'Raewat'. Is it a mere coincidence? We will have to wait till we are absolutely clear about the meaning of the other word that is paired with it. Of all different versions of the word, 'XarvanaMuhatO' seems to be the most appropriate transcription. It is found in the Gatha, which is the earliest Zoroastrian scripture. 'XarvanaMuhatO' is not a single word. It is a compound word made up of 'Xarvanam' and 'Uhato'. 'Xarvanam' is identically found in both languages. In Sanskrit, it means – 'to flow down' or 'to trickle down'. 'Uhato' in both languages means – 'arise'or 'appear'. If we take the word 'raEwatO' to be the name of some mountain then, in such case, the meaning of 'raEwatO XarvanaMuhatO' becomes –

'It arises (or appears) - flowing down the Mountain RaEwat'.

In Zoroastrian hymns, 'kharenanghacha (Xarvanam cha)' is, quite often, also preceded with-'Ahe raya'.Observe the following hymn of Khordeh Avesta–

Ahe raya kharenanghacha[1]

We get the same line in Ardui Sur Bano Yasht of Khordeh Avesta. But here things are written somewhat differently. Observe the hymn of Ardui Sur Bano Yasht –

Ahe raya Xarvnamhaca[2]

Each and every word of this hymn is found identically in Sanskrit as well.In Sanskrit, the meaning of each word of this hymn can be summarized as follows

Ahe (Asi) – To be

Raya – stream, river, current of flowing water

Kharenanghacha (Xarvanamcha) – trickle down

1 Khordeh Avesta – Ardibehesht Yasht – para – (18).

2 Khordeh Avesta – Ardui Sur Bano Yasht – para – (9).

Even in Avesta, it should have exactly similar meaning. These are the words that are found identically – in both languages. Therefore, we may take it for granted that these words were there in the world of P-I-E speaking Aryans. They got assimilated directly in both languages – in exactly similar form and with exactly similar meaning. These words are still there in modern Sanskrit. And they are no different in form, as well as meaning – from Vedic Sanskrit. These words have been there since thousands of years. They existed even before Aryan migration started. They are still alive – in exactly identical form – in Sanskrit. We know what these words meant initially. They carry the same meaning even today – in Sanskrit. But Avesta became extinct long back. The Avestan words were assigned specific meanings at some later stage. It was here that differences cropped in. We know what these words meant in the Vedic world. Even today – their meaning remains unchanged. These words must have meant the same when Avestan hymns were compiled. It was only at some later stage that, in Persia, some new meanings were attributed to these words.The meaning of 'xarvanam' (kharenangha) is absolutely clear. It could never be something like 'radiant' or 'possessed of glory'. Observe that this line is there in 'Ardui Sur Bano Yasht '. This 'raya' – stream or river - is none other than Ardvi Sur. 'Xarvanam Uhato' of Zoroastrian texts exactly stands for – 'to arise or appear flowing down'.

And now we come to another mythical word – Tishtra. Tishtra literally means – three. However, in both Vedic and Avestan mythology, Tishtra carries a different connotation. In Vedas, Tishtra is the common name given to the three sacred rivers – Ida, Bharati and Saraswati. In laterAvestan texts too, Tishtra is associated with the three rivers – Arang, Veh and Marv. It is interesting to note that 'Ida' and 'Bharati' are not the rivers of Sapt-Sindhu region. Similarly, Arang, Veh and

Marv can not be identified with any of the rivers of Iran. And why would Vedic Aryans pick up a group of just three rivers – and deify them differently? Their region had seven equally important rivers. And why would they not include the most important river – Indus – in that group? Things are precisely clear. This concept of the deity – Tishtra – was brought to both worlds by migrating Aryans. Tishtra – got assimilated in like fashion in Vedic and Avestan mythology. In original homeland of Aryans – Tishtra must have been the deity related with three rivers. However, at some later stage, Aryans of Persia gave it a different meaning. They started explaining Tishtra as – the star Sirius. But let us observe the following hymn of Khordeh Avesta that gives out more information about Tishtra–

tiStryO raEwI XarvnaMuhi[1]
zryaMhat haca WourukaCAT

It says – the Tishtra (three rivers) – arise trickling down the Mountain Raewat. But here, we can clearly identify one of them. One of them is definitely the River of Vourukash. Ardvi Sur appeared in this world trickling down the Mountain Raewat. Avestan texts also describe that – of the three – it is only Ardvi Sur that trickles down from the southern slope of the Mountain. That is exactly how even Narmada rises – trickling down the southern slope of Vindhyas.

Avestan texts do not eulogize or deify any other river. Zoroastrian world revolved only around 'Ardvi Sur'. Could it be that Raewat was the most important mountain peak of Zoroastrian world? But the Raewat Mountain of Zoroastrian scripture, which is believed to be in Khorasan, has no river. However, we have earlier identified this river of Vourukash as the river Narmada of Bharooch. Let us see where our Narmada

1 Khordeh Avesta – Tishtar Yasht – para – (32).

originates from. River Narmada is mentioned in Rig Veda. But there is no hymns in Rig Veda that can help us locate its place of origin. However, in Skand Puran (Reva Khand) we do come across two mythological stories that contain information about its place of origin. At one place we are told that, when the great Sage Pururuwa brought river Narmada down on to this earth from heaven, no mountain peak volunteered to become the base to receive this mighty river. At the end, it was Mount Paryank of Vindhyan Ranges which offered its services willingly and became the base of the heavenly river on this planet. And at another place, we are told that river Narmada was brought on this earth by the Sage Hiranyateja. Earlier it existed in heaven and, when it descended down, the Northern Udayachal Mountain became its base on earth. These mythological references of Skand Puran are somewhat ambiguous and we can not conclude anything. Could it be that Mount Paryank and Northern Udayachal Mountain were two different names of the same peak? But things become further confusing when we find in the famous epic Mahabharata that river Narmada originates from the Mahendragiri Mountain. We are also told that another name of Narmada is Mekal-Suta. It is so because Narmada originates from the Mountain Mekal and hence, it is called the daughter of Mount Mekal. 'Suta' literally means – daughter. Mount Mekal is identified with modern 'Amarkantak' of Vindhyan Ranges. Thus we find so many different names of the mountain peak from where Narmada originates. But nowhere do we come across the mention of Raewat.

However, let us find out where the Raewat Mountain of Indian mythology is located. It will be interesting to find if any river originates from its peaks. 'Brahma Purana' gives out the names of seven most important mountain ranges of India. They are – Mahendra, Malaya, Sahya, Shuktiman,

Rkshwat, Vindhya and Pariyatra. Almost all religious texts of Hinduism confirm these names of important ranges of India. But nowhere do we get the mention of 'Raewat'. Could it be that 'Raewat' was no different from 'Rkshwat'? Could it be that 'Raewat' was, in ancient days, the colloquial variation of 'Rkshwat'? I think so. According to some Puranas the river Narmada originates from Rkshwat Mountain, which is also considered as the eastern spur of Vindhya Mountain. Even Valmiki Ramayana (6-18-10) links Narmada with the Rkshwat. Valmiki Ramayan also gives out the names of the tribal people who lived in the regions of Rkshwat Mountain. In 'Kishkindha Kand' of Valmiki Ramayan it is said that the forests of Rkshwat were guarded by five 'Gandharwas'. They were Shailuka, Gramani, Shuka, Shiksha and Bavru. Thus, we come to know about Bavru or Bavra people. They were inhabitants of area surrounding the Mountain Rkshwat. Interestingly, even in Avestan texts as well as in Vedas, we find the mention of these Bavra people. Observe the following hymn -

bvrvzatO ahurahe nafvDro[1]

The Avestan word 'zato' is identically found in Sansrit, where it stands for – tribe or caste. Here, 'Bvrvzato' can be translated as – the people belonging to Bavra caste. The Avestan word 'nafvDro' means – grand children. Its corresponding identical word in Sanskrit is – 'naptri' or 'napat'. In Sanskrit also, 'naptri' stands for – grand children of sons and daughters. The hymn declares –

> People belonging to Bavra zati (caste) are direct descendents (grand children) of Lord Ahura himself.

Isn't this bewildering? We have seen earlier that Lord Ahura was none other than the Sun God. In Hindu mythology too, we have somewhat similar reference. In Sanskrit, we have

1 Gatha – Yasna – 3 – para – (7).

a word – 'Suryavanshi'. 'Suryavanshi' is a compound word – made up of 'Surya' and 'Vanshi'. 'Surya' is the Sun God and 'Vanshi' stands for lineal-relation. 'Suryavanshi' exactly means – having lineal relations with Sun God or descendents of Sun God. Thus, 'Ahurahe Nafvdro' of Avestan texts and the 'Suryavanshi' of later Vedic mythology are no different. Could it be that Bavra people were the earliest 'Suryavanshi'? It is interesting to note that all rulers of the famous kingdom of 'Ayodhya', of Indian mythology, were from 'Suryavanshi' clan. And 'Lord Rama' was the most important of them all. Now observe the following Avestan line of Zoroastrian Gatha –

bvrvzaitIm amawaitIm huraoD&m[1]

'Bavrvzaitim' is a compound word made up of 'Bavrv' and 'Zaitim'. 'Bavrv' stands for the name of the caste or class of people. The root word of 'Zaitim' is 'Zati' i.e. caste. Thus, 'Bvrvzaitim' can be translated as – 'the Bavra caste' or 'the people belonging to Bavra caste'. 'Amawaitim' is the name of a place. It is 'Amavart'. This word has been discussed in detail in the following chapter. 'Huraod&m' is the Avestan word for daughter. The hymn says – 'people belonging to Bavra caste are considered as the true daughters of Amavart'.

But let us come back to river Ardvi Sur. There is an interesting relation between Ardvi Sur, Narmada and Haoma (Soma). We know that Avestan Haoma (Vedic Soma) was the name of a plant from which intoxicating elixir was obtained. Even the elixir thus obtained was also called Soma or Haoma. It was generally believed that Soma (Haoma) plant used to grow on the high mountain peaks of Tian-Shan, Paamir and Himalayas. These are the places where, even today, the best variety of Ephedra is found. It was taken for granted that Haoma was nothing but a potent variety of Ephedra. But this

1 Gatha – Yasna – 2 – para – (14).

is not true. We find innumerable references of Soma (Haoma) in both Vedic and Avestan texts. Yasna – 9 to 11 of Avestan Gatha is dedicated to Haoma and it is very significant to observe that, even in Rig-Veda, Chapter - 9 is dedicated to Soma. Could it be just co-incidence? Could it be that Gatha is no different from Vedas? Can we say that Gatha is but the Fifth Veda? Right now nothing can be said conclusively about it but, according to 'Nirukta', Rig, Hotra and Gatha are words with exactly similar meanings. They are synonyms. In this context, we have an interesting Avestan hymn.

WIspaEca paNca gAqI[1]

The hymn declares that, altogether, there were five Gathas, in this world. Could it be that the four Vedas were nothing but the remaining four Gathas? The second and third hymn of Chapter 146 of 'Shantiparva' in the epic 'Mahabharata' gives out the true meaning of the word – 'Gatha'. Here, 'Gatha', 'Yagyagatha' (hymns related with Yagya ceremony), and 'Shloka' are considered synonyms. Even in Sam Veda, the meaning of 'Gatha' is some what similar. Observe the following hymn of Sam Veda –

Vipraaya gaatham gaayat yam jujoshate[2]

Here, 'Gatham' is believed to stand for – 'the holy hymns of Veda'. In this hymn of Sam Veda, wise men are asked to recite the sacred hymns of Vedas, which are so pleasing to Lord Indra. In all probability, initially, hymns of Gatha were no different from the Shlokas of Vedas. Observe another hymn of Atharv Veda which throws light on this subject –

Aasnaste gaatha shramavannushnisamvo balam vashe[3]

1 Gatha – Yasna – 71 – para – (6).
2 Sam Veda – Chapter – IV – (446).
3 Atharv Veda – 10 – 10 – (20).

It says – 'the 'Gatha' has sprung from your mouth and the 'Power' from your neck'. Now observe the following hymn of Atharva Veda (2006) –

Idamugraya bavrawe namo

It says –'we revere the violent Bavra people'.

But let us come back to the relation between Ardvi Sur, Narmada and Haoma. Ardvi Sur must have been the river around which existed the predecessors of ancient Avesta speaking Iranians. But where was it? Could it be identified with river Narmada? I think so. River Narmada is also called – 'Somodbhava'. Literally, Somodbhava means – arising or originating from (the land or area of) Soma. It almost gives out exact location of Haoma. Another name of Narmada is – 'Somasuta' i.e. 'the daughter of Soma'. Could it be that the mountain peaks, from where originates river Narmada, were abode of the famous Haoma plants? Could it be that the mountain of Bavra people - Rkshwat – was the place of sacred Haoma? Avestan texts describe the land of Haoma or Soma as –

staomi garayO bvrvzaNtO[1]
yaqra haoma urUruDuCa

This hymn gives out the exact location where Avestan Haoma was found. 'staomi' is – to pray, to revere. Here the root word is – 'Stu'. Even in Sanskrit 'Stu' has exactly similar meaning. In Sanskrit also, the word 'Stu' or 'Stuti' stands for – revere, eulogise, pray. Avestan word 'Garayo' is identically found in Sanskrit as well. It stands for – mountain. Even in Sanskrit, 'Giri' is mountain or hill feature. 'Bvrvzanto' exactly stands for Bavra people or the land or region of Bavra people. . Avestan 'yaqra' is the corresponding identical of Sanskrit 'yatra'. It stands for – where. In Avestan texts the meaning of

1 Gatha – Yasna – 10 - para - (3).

'urUruDuCa' is given as – to grow. Even in Sanskrit the word 'Ruh' and/or 'Rurh' is found with exactly similar meaning. In Sanskrit also 'Ruh' is – to grow. Thus, the aforesaid hymn of can be translated as –

We revere the mountains of Bavra people
Where Haoma grows (where Haoma is found)

The hymn gives out the place where Soma plants were found. It used to grow on the mountain peaks of Bavra people. Bavra people lived around the Mountain Rkshwat. Haoma grew on Rkshwat Mountain. And river Narmada still flows through the regions of Rkshwat. No wonder that river Narmada was called – 'Somodbhava' and 'Somsuta'. About this, there is an interesting line in Bundahishn texts of Mazdayasni religion. Observe the following lines of Bundahishn –

'And near to that tree, the white Haoma, the healing and undefiled,
has grown at the source of the water of Aredvi Sur…….[1]'

There we are! Ardvi Sur is none other than Narmada. Haoma grows at the place of origin of river Ardvi Sur. Ardvi Sur, too, is – 'Somodbhava'. Ardvi Sur arises from the land of Soma. It is none other than – 'Somsuta'- the daughter of Soma. This river must have originated from the mountain peaks of 'Rkshwat', where ancient Bavra people used to live. Now observe the following lines of Yasna – 22 of Gatha –

raEwato XarvnaMuhatO amvCan&m spvNtan&m[2]
Imvm haomvm aCaya uzdAtvm Ayese Yesti

'Raewato Xarvnamuhato' is as usual – arising or appearing flowing down the Raewat Mountain. 'amvCan&m' (pronounced as 'amvashanam') is the corresponding identical

1 Bundahishn - Chapter 27 – (4).
2 Gatha – Yasna – 22 – para – (1).

of Sanskrit – 'ambhasanam'. Here, the root word is 'ambhas' which is 'water' or 'water-body'. 'spvNtan&m' can be translated as – purifying, consecrating. Here the root word is – 'pav'. Even in Sanskrit – 'pav' or 'pavati' means the same. 'Imvm haomvm' is – 'this Haoma'. 'aCaya' means 'here' and 'uzdAtvm' is - 'to grow'. 'Ayese Yesti' stands for – 'So it is'. Thus, the whole hymn can be translated as –

This consecrating water-mass arises,
trickling down the Mountain Raewat,
and here grow these Haoma plants.
So it is.

The abode of famous Haoma plants was the Mountain Raewat. And the consecrating waters of Ardvi Sur trickled down the Raewat Mountain. Ardvi Sur is none other than Narmada.

In all probability, Bavras were the common ancestors of Avesta speaking ancient Iranians and people belonging to Vedic civilization. Zoroastrians of early days were familiar with the place where Soma plants grew. They knew it was found in a different land. They knew that the mountain peak, where Haoma grew, was situated in the world of Bavra people. They worshipped Haoma. They worshipped the mountains of Bavra people. And they also worshipped and eulogized the river of Bavra people. It was Ardvi Sur. It was no different from Narmada. No wonder they used to say – 'dUrAT haca ahmAT daiNghaoT' (far away is situated our home land). Now we know why Avestan texts do not accord more importance even to river Indus. Ardvi Sur i.e. Narmada was the most important river of their ancestors. Bavra people were the common ancestors of Indo-Iranians. Aryans never came to India and Iran from some other country. They were descendents of Bavra people. Observe the following hymn of Sam Veda -

Puruni bavro ni charanti[1]

Observe that, even in this hymn of Sam Veda, 'bavro' is preceded by 'puruni', which stands for 'old' or 'ancient'. Bavra people were the predecessors of Vedic Aryans as well as Avesta speaking ancient Iranians. Now observe the following hymn of Sam Veda –

Ta gaathayaa puraanyaa punaanambhyanooshat[2]

The hymn says – 'they worship the holy Soma by singing grand old commonly used prayers.' Here, 'Gatha' is explained as prayers that were common; hymns that were often used to propitiate the divinities. Observe that, here also, Gatha is reffered to as something – 'puraanyaa'. The word 'puraanyaa' literally means – old, antique, ancient. Thus we find the mention of 'Gatha' and 'Bavra' in Vedic texts as well. In Vedas, they are often described as something old, ancient or pre-existng. And this is the truth. Bavra civilization was pre-Vedic. Bavra civilization was pre-Zorastrian. Bavra people were common ancestors of both Vedic Aryans and ancient Zoroastrians of Iran. 'Bavra' literally means – uneducated, uncivilized, tribal. 'Arya' is the antonym of 'Bavra'. 'Arya' literally stands for – civilized, educated. These two words reveal all about our Indo-Iranian civilization. It was agriculture that heralded the new Aryan civilization. The process of Aryanization started with advent of agriculture. And it happened in Bavra world. It happened first, in Narmada Valley, which was the abode of Bavra people. It happened around Rkshwat Mountain. Aryans never came to India and Iran, from some other part of the world. Aryan was not a different race. They never came with some Proto-Indo-European (P-I-E) language. Rather, Bavra people had a distinct language of their own which, with the

1 Sam Veda – Chapter – V – (516).
2 Sam Veda – Chapter – XVII – (1633).

passage of time, evolved to become languages like Avesta, Sanskrit, Pali etc. All these languages are so closely similar. And yet, they bear the fact that none of them is the direct descendent of the other. It is so because all of them have had common root. They all evolved from the single source. Now we know why even language Pali does not seem to be direct descendent of Sanskrit.

Therefore, before we proceed further, let us arrange our findings in a logical sequence. They are as follows –

1. Bavras lived in the region around Rakshwat Mountain.
2. The mountain peaks of Bavra people were abode of famous Haoma (Soma) plants.
3. Avestan texts also reveal the fact that Soma plants grew at the source of river Ardvi Sur. Therefore, we may conclude that river Ardvi Sur must have originated from the same mountain peaks of Bavra world, which was the abode of rare Haoma plants.
4. But we are told that river Ardvi Sur arises flowing down the Mountain Raewat.
5. Therefore, Raewat Mountain is none other than the Rakshwat Mountain of Bavra people.
6. As on date, it is river Narmada that flows down the Rakshwat Mountain.
7. Therefore, river Ardvi Sur of Avestan texts is none other than river Narmada of modern days.
8. Avestan texts describe that river Ardvi Sur marks or flows through the centre of the world. River Narmada flows precisely through the centre of the Indian subcontinent.

9. Haoma grows near the source of river Ardvi Sur. Ardvi Sur is none other than Narmada. River Narmada is also called 'Some-suta' (daughter of Soma) and 'Somodbhva' (originating from the land of Soma).
10. Observe how easily 'Namo-Ardvebhyo', when recited repeatedly, tends to become 'Narmadebhyo'.
11. Avestan texts describe that River Ardvi Sur flows on the grounds of 'Vourukash'. They also reveal existence of Sea of Vourukash. River Narmada actually flows on the grounds of 'Varukaksha' and falls into the Sea of Varukaksha which, these days, is called Arabian Sea.

Now, let us explain the previous hymn of Yasna – 24 that says '*ahurahe mazdI raEwatO XarvanaMuhatO*'. It is quite simple. In the light of the Avestan hymns, Ahura is considered as the giver of Mazda. He is called – 'mazdadhata'.

Observe the following line of Gatha –

mazdI dAyAT ahurO[1]

It says – Mazda is given by Lord Ahura. In Avestan scriptures, Ahura is used to convey either the Sun itself or the deity whose most significant physical manifestation is the Sun. In Sanskrit, the corresponding identical word of 'Mazda' is 'medha'. Literally, 'medha' can be defined as – brightness or brilliance. That is what even the Avestan 'mazda' is. 'Ahurahe Mazdi' is 'the brilliance or bright rays of the Sun God – Lord Ahura'. Thus, the aforesaid hymn can be translated exactly as–

The bright rays of the Sun (Ahura),
appear cascading down the mountain Raewat.'

1 Gatha –Yasna – 43 – para – (1).

Ancient Bavra people must have observed the brightness of dawn, coming down each morning, from the peaks of Mountain Raewat. Its foot hills were their home land. Similarly, ' daquCo ahurahe mazdI raEwatO XrvnaMuhatO' can be translated as –

> The bright rays, which is given by the Sun (Ahura),
> appear cascading down the Mountain Raewat.

In Indian mythology too, the Sun is believed to arise each morning from behind the Udayachal Mountain. And we know that Udayachal is another name of the same peak from where Narmada originates.

However, this deification of river Ardvi Sur i.e. Narmada by ancient Aryans of Iran speaks volumes about the place of origin of Aryans. Now we may rightly conclude that, on the banks of Narmada, must have flourished the earliest civilization of mankind. It must have been the cradle of Aryan culture. Here began the process of Aryanization. Narmada-Valley must have been the original home of Aryans. It was from here that they branched off to different parts of the world. No matter where they went; no matter what they became; they remained ever indebted to this holy river. It had sustained their predecessors. Its water was considered as nectar that provided fertility to the lands, where mankind sowed first crops. She was also considered the Goddess of Fertility. But, with passage of time, the knowledge of its existence was lost in Persia. Ardvi Sur had become a deity. They could no more relate it to the river that still flowed along the central latitude of India; that still poured down from the high peaks of Raewat (Rkshwat), flowing all the way towards Bharooch (Vourukash).

Now, let us observe some remaining lines of Yasna – 65.

They reveal significant information.

HukairyAT haca barvzaMhaT[1]
Aoi zrayO Wouru-kaCvm

The meaning of each word can be summarized as follows–

Hukairyat---from great heights
Ha cha---too
Barezanghat--- banging fiercely (against stones)
Aoizrayo(Avizrayo)---coming towards, flowing towards
WourukaCvm (Vourukashem)---Vourukash

In some Avestan texts, 'Aoizrayo' is often transcribed as – 'Avizrayo'. The whole passage can be translated as – 'falling from great heights and banging fiercely (against stones), it comes all the way towards Vourukash'. But here, the most important word is – 'avizrayo'. It will be interesting to understand the meaning of word 'avizrayo' properly, as it is going to speak volumes. 'Avizraya' is opposite of 'pravazraya'. 'Pravazraya' stands for – going away. 'Pravazraya' was a common practice of Buddhist and Jaina monks of ancient India. It involved wandering about from place to place. It was a state of home-less-ness. They were people without permanent residence. 'Pravazrya' never envisaged any proper destination. But 'avizraya' is exactly opposite of 'pravazraya'. It always refers to some place or destination towards which the person is coming. Here, in this hymn, this focal point is Vourukash. The river is described as coming all the way to Vourukash.

But this use of 'avizraya' presupposes that the writer of these lines had to be present physically in and around Vourukash. Only then could he describe the river as coming towards Vourukash. Consider a man cycling to a school. All other observers will say that the man is going to the school.

1 Yasna – 65 – para – (3).

However, the students who are physically present in the school premises will describe it differently. They will not say that the man is going to school. They will say – the man is coming to school. Thus, from any other geographical location the river would appear to be 'going towards' Vourukash. From nowhere else, can it be described as coming towards Vourukash. Persons of Vourukash alone could use the word 'avizraya'. What does it signify? Was the text compiled here? Was 'Vourukash', in those ancient days, the most important center of activities of the followers of Mazdayasni or Zoroastrian religion? With meager knowledge that we possess today, we are not in position to say any thing about that. But centuries later, when Zoroastrians decided to migrate from Iran, they came and settled in and around Bharooch. It was not a mere coincidence. It was their Vourukash. Their homecoming was yet another 'avizraya'. They had come back to their home land which, in those grand old days, was called – 'Amavart'.

AMAVANT

Apo ishtim vo jaidhyami pouru saredham amavaitim[1]

This is a hymn from 'Ardvi Sur Niyaesh' of Khordeh Avesta. In Avestan religious texts, it is translated as – 'O Waters, I beseech happiness through you, with plenty of courage and self supporting off-springs'. I do not know what made them explain things in such manner. Let us try and understand the true meaning of this Avestan hymn. We know that, of all Zoroastrian scriptures, Gatha is the oldest. It is believed that a large number of hymns of Gatha were compiled by none other than Zoroaster himself. All other Avestan texts are of relatively much later dates and many hymns of Gatha are incorporated in these scriptures of later periods. It is interesting to note that the aforesaid hymn of Khordeh Avesta is also derived from Gatha. We come across the same line in Yasna 65 of the Gatha too. But there we find things written somewhat differently. In Gatha, 'pouru saredham' is written as 'pouru-sarvadm'. Since Gatha is the earliest text of Zoroastrians, we will consider its hymns to be the original ones. In later Avestan books, they were, at times, adopted erroneously. Let us analyze the true meaning of this hymn. We know that 'sarvadm' is an Avestan as well as Sanskrit word for – always. Similarly, 'pouru' is again a common word found in both languages. It stands for 'predecessors' or 'ancient'. I do not know what lead them to believe that 'jaidhyami' could mean 'beseech'. Its root word is – 'jai'. Both in Avesta and Sanskrit, the word denotes an act of prayer or worship. 'Water' and 'water bodies' were worshipped even by Zoroaster. 'Apo jaiDyOiS ZaraquStra' is a line from Yasna 65 of Gatha. It says

1 Khordeh Avesta – Ardvi Sur Niyaesh – para – (11).

– 'Zoroaster offers his salutations to the waters'. 'ishtim' is also found identically in both languages. It can be translated as – a thing or person that is revered or worshipped or praise worthy. Here, 'ishtim' is an adjective qualifying the word 'Apo' i.e. water. 'Apo' is water in Avesta as well as in Sanskrit. 'Apo ishtim' can be translated as – waters, worthy of reverence. Like all other ancient civilizations, 'water' and 'water bodies' were worshipped in Zoroastrian world too. In both languages, 'vo' stands for – whom or which. Thus, 'Apo ishtim vo jaidhyami pouru sarvadm' can be exactly translated as –

This water, which was always worshipped by our predecessors, is great and worthy of reverence.

'Amavaitim' is the only word that is not found identically in Sanskrit language. Zoroastrian religious texts explain 'amavaitim' as strength or courage. They believe that the root word here is 'amawant', which is the corresponding identical of the Pahlavi word 'amavand'. In Pahlavi, 'amavand' stands for courage. But if we take that to be the true meaning of 'amavant' then the meaning of the aforesaid hymn becomes absurd. If 'amavaitim' is 'courage' then the meaning of the aforesaid hymn becomes –

> This water, which was always worshipped by our predecessors courageously, is great and worthy of reverence.

That doesn't sound reasonable. Worship is an act that emanates from deep faith. Courage is unwarranted in any act of worship. It is ridiculous to presume that, to worship waters, great effort and courage was required by the predecessors. In those glorious days, rivers and water bodies were deified all over. Observe the following lines of 'Ardvi Sur Niyaesh' of Khordeh Avesta, which deals with reverence that was offered to the waters of the world –

Ma no Apo dush-mananghe[1]
Ma no Apo dush- vachanghe
Ma no Apo dush-shyaothnai'

Avestan texts translate these lines as – 'Our waters are not for the evil minded, our waters are not for the evil speakers, our waters are not for the evil doers'. It was a warning to humanity to preserve the holiness of water and not to contaminate it. Observe another hymn of Zoroastrian Gatha -

Ap&mcA xI YazamaidE[2]
Ap&mcA pvrvtUS YazamaidE

'Xi' and 'pvrvtUs' are Sanskrit as well as Avestan words for 'sky' and 'mountain' respectively. The lines can be translated as –

We worship, hereby, the waters of the sky
We worship, hereby, the waters of the mountains

Thus, we may reasonably conclude that courage had nothing to do with an act that involved worship of rivers and water bodies by our predecessors. It was so natural on their part. Their civilization was indebted to the waters of Ardvi Sur. Hence, to sincerely reciprocate, they deified it. Water bodies were worshipped all over. It was spontaneous and natural. In those ancient days, people did not need courage to offer prayers of reverence to waters. Therefore, 'amavaitim' could not be courage or strength.

Observe the following Hymn of Yasna 48 of Zoroastrian Gatha –

AmvrvtAitI daEwAiScA maKyAiScA[3]

1 Khordeh Avesta – Ardvi Sur Niyaesh – para – (7).
2 Gatha – Yasna – 42 – para – (1).
3 Gatha – Yasna – 48 – para – (1).

In Avestan Texts 'Amavaitim' is also written as 'Amvrvtaitim'. At different places, they are transcribed differently. 'daEwAiS' and 'makyAiS' of Avestan Gatha can be translated as – the divinities and the mortals. However, there is a misconception about the meaning of Avestan word 'Daeva'. Followers of Zoroastrianism generally believe that Avestan 'Daeva' stands for – Demons and false Gods. I have dealt with this misconception in Chapter – 5 of this book. 'DaEwAiS'-MakyAiS' is the corresponding identical of 'Daeva – Martya' of Vedic texts, which stands for – 'Gods and Mortals'. If we consider 'AmvrvtAitI' to be 'courage' then the meaning of the aforesaid Hymn becomes absurd again. 'Courageous Gods or Divinities' is certainly an uncommon expression. 'AmvrvtAitI' could be any thing but 'courage'.

Let us analyze what else could possibly be the true meaning of 'amavaitim'. We often come across words in Avestan scriptures where Sanskrit 'r' becomes silent and is replaced by 'ai'. In Zoroastrian religious texts, we find 'prati' always and invariably written as 'paiti'. 'Paiti' is the corresponding identical of the Sanskrit word – 'prati'. Could it be that 'amavaitim' of this Avestan hymn is the corresponding identical of the Sanskrit word 'amavartim'? Here the root word could be 'amavart'. 'Amavart' literally means – the land of rivers. There we are! Could it be the specific name of some place or land? No wonder that, 'Amavaitim' is, at different places, also transcribed as 'Amvrvtaitim', which is so close to the root word – 'Amavart'.

But the most amazing thing about earliest Avestan scriptures is that they do not mention any place, river or geographical feature of Iran. The names like Persia or Iran is just not there. Till date, no one knows by what name the ancient Zoroastrians called their home land. Was there no name at all? It seems quite unnatural. Zoroastrians have had a rich civilization. They had a distinct well-knit social structure. Their religious philosophy was vibrant with pragmatism. They gave to the world the idea of life after death and doctrine of divine punishment and reward. They evolved the concept of heaven and hell.

They were the first to start the practice of offering prayers five times a day. Almost all existing religions of today's world are – in some way or the other – indebted to this rich Zoroastrian faith. How could they not have a name for their country? It is simply unbelievable. It has to be there in the texts as well. It is so inevitable.

Avestan hymns mention about the masters of villages. They called them 'vishpaitim'. The word 'vish' is identically found in Sanskrit and Avesta. It stands for – village. Similarly, they mention about masters of towns whom they called 'zantupaitim'. Thus, it may be concluded that Avestan society had both villages and towns. However, it is significant to observe that they even had fair idea of a nation. The Avestan word – 'danghubyo' stands for 'nation' or 'country'. And yet, we do not get the name of that country in any of the Zoroastrian texts. In Yasna 67 of Avestan Gatha, they declared – 'dUrAt haca ahmAT daNghaoT (far away is situated our country)'. It proves that they did have concept of a nation or country. It also proves that they had left their country long back. But what did they call it? Why did they not assigne any name to their nation? Although, in Avestan texts, this home land of ancient Zoroastrians is often referred to as – 'aryamno danghubyo'. 'Aryamno danghubyo' exactly means – 'the country of Aryans'. However, 'Aryamno danghubyo' is not a name. It is a descriptive expression of identification of a particular geographical entity. 'Aryamno danghubyo' is not a proper noun. It is not some thing like 'Iran' or 'Aryavart'. It is significant to observe that both these words are translated exactly similarly. 'Iran' and 'Aryavart' literally mean – country of Aryans. But unlike 'Aryamno danghubyo', Iran and Aryavart are proper nouns. They are names. But none of these names are ever mentioned in Zoroastrian texts. 'Aryamno danghubyo' could not be the name of their country.

On many occasions, through out Zoroastrian texts, this home land of Avesta speaking people of ancient days is also referred to as – 'Ramno Kshatrahe'. This can be translated as – 'the country of Rama' or 'the land of Rama'. However, in Avestan texts, it is translated as – 'the good land', where the meaning of 'ramno' is considered to be 'good' and 'Kshatrahe' is 'land'. 'Ramno Kshatrahe Yazam Ide' can be found frequently throughout Zoroastrian texts. According to their religious scriptures its exact meaning is – 'we revere, hereby, the good land'. But 'Ramno kshatrahe' is, again, not a name. It is an expression exactly similar to 'Aryamno danghubyo'. Just like 'Aryamno danghubyo', even 'Ramno kshatrahe' is not a proper noun. Therefore, even 'Ramno Kshatrahe' could not have been the name of Avestan world.

We know that Narmada – Valley was the home land of earliest Zoroastrians. From here, they had migrated to different parts of world. The conspicuous absence of names of places, rivers or geographical features of Iran also confirms that most of the Avestan hymns were not compiled in Iran. 'Kellen' was close to truth when he suggested that the language Avesta was not a language of Iran. Could it be that even Avesta was an Indian language and that the earliest Avestan hymns were compiled here, in India? That could be the reason why these hymns mention only about Indian places. In Zoroastrian scriptures we often come across names of Gokarn, Varukaksha, Gaya, Sapta-Sindhu, Raewat Mountain and Ardvi Sur (Narmada). On the other hand, Avestan texts do not mention any of the places, rivers or mountains of Persia.

However, we do get some very interesting facts that are related with the original homeland of ancient Iranians. The Avestan scriptures reveal to us that the country of Avesta speaking people had six well defined seasons. Therefore, we may conclude that it could not be Iran. Iran is a country with only four distinct seasons. Also, the original homeland of Avesta speaking people was characterized by seven distinct mountain ranges. There is an interesting hymn on this subject –

GairIScA afStacinO YazamaidE[1]

'GairIS' is as usual, 'mountains' or 'mountain – ranges'. Even in Sanskrit 'Giri' means the same. 'Yazamaide' is 'Yazam ide'. It stands for – 'We revere, hereby'. 'cinO' (pronounced as 'chino') can be translated as – 'mount'. We find its meaning explained in para – 13 of Chapter – 12 of Bundahishn, where it is the nama of a mountain. 'afSta' is the erroneous transcription of – 'safta', which is the corresponding identical of the Sanskrit word – 'sapta'. It denotes the number – seven. In Avestan texts, we come across many instances where words are not transcribed strictly in accordance with the way they are pronounced. And the reason is obvious. By the time these hymns were transcribed in Pahalvi script, the language Avesta had become extinct. Even the script and the language of hymns were mismatched. That is the reason why some words got transcribed erroneously. In Yasna – 30 of Avestan texts, we come across – 'vrvS WIKyAtA'. It is the erroneous transcription of – 'Srv WIKyAtA' which is the corresponding identical of 'sarv wikhyata' of Sanskrit. We know that 'WIKyAtA' or 'wikhyat' means – 'famous'. 'WIKyAtA' or 'wikhyat' can only be preceeded by something like – 'sarv'. 'Sarv WIKyAtA' exactly means – whose name and fame reached far and wide.

1 Gatha – Yasna – 42 – para – (2).

Similarly, 'afstcino' is the erroneous transcription of – 'saptcino'.Thus, 'GairimcA afstcino yazamaide' can be translated as – 'We revere, hereby, the peaks of the seven mountain ranges'. We know that it refers to none other place. Only Indian Subcontinent is characterized by seven distinct mountain ranges. It is a fact that is attested by almost all scriptures of Hinduism. And they are – Mahendra, Malaya, Sahya, Shuktiman, Rkshwat, Vindhya and Pariyatra.

But let us come back again to our main querry. Why do the Avestan hymns not reveal the name of the country? What was the name of the nation to which ancient Zoroastrians belonged? We are familiar with many ancient names of India. Aryavart, Brahmavart, Dhilmun and Jambudwip are some of the earliest known names of this country. Vedic people called it – Aryavart. But Avestan hymns do not contain any of these names. Should we conclude that Avestan hymns were compiled anytime before India was called Aryavart? Could it be that in those early days, India was called – Amavart (the land of rivers)? Let us analyse, once again, the following Avestan line of Yasna – 2 of Zoroastrian Gatha –

BvrvzaitIm amawaitIm huraoD&m[1]

It can be translated as – 'the caste Bavra is considered as the true daughters of Amavart'. 'Huraod&m' is the Avestan word for daughter. 'Bavrvzaitim' is a compound word. It is made up of 'Bavrv' and 'Zaitim'. 'Bavrv' stands for the name of a caste or class of people. The root word of 'Zaitim' is 'Zati' i.e. caste. Bavra were people who lived in Narmada Valley. In the days of Zoroaster, Arya and Bavra way of living existed side by side. Zoroastrian era was a period of transition. But Bavra people were considered the original natives of this country. Advent of agriculture and process of

1 Gatha – Yasna – 2 – para – (14).

aryanization was a phenomenon of later days. Bavras were the predeccessors of Aryans. The Hymn is dedicated to them. It declares the significance of original inhabitants of this country. Bavra people are called true daughters of the soil of Amavart. In those early days, daughters of the soil were more important than sons of the soil. Bavra society was matriarchal. Sons of the soil were insignificant. People worshipped Gods to bless them with female child. The Hymn declares in no uncertain words that the Bavra people were true daughters of the soil of Amavart. In the days of Zoroaster, India was called Amavart. Therefore, 'apo ishtim vo jaidhyami pouru sarvadm amawaitim' can now be exactly translated as -

This water, which was always worshipped by our predecessors in Amavart, is great and worthy of reverence'.

There was a characteristic Avestan rule of incorporating 'n' in certain words. We find occasions where 'Ahu' becomes 'Anhu' and 'Vohu' becomes 'Vanhu' in Avesta. Similarly, the colloquial variation of Amavart became – 'Amavant'. In Zoroastrian hymns, on several occasions, Amavart is written as Amavant also. It was the name of the country where most of the Avestan hymns were compiled. Observe another Avestan line where the river of Vourukash is described –

Yao zema paiti fratachaiti[1]
Ya amavaiti fratachaiti

It is important to observe that, even in these lines, Avestan 'paiti' is nothing but corresponding identical of the Sanskrit word – 'prati'. 'Yao zema paiti fratachaiti' can be translated as – which falls on the ground (earth). 'Zema' is earth or ground. 'Fratachaiti' is the corresponding identical of 'pratachaiti' of Sanskrit. In both languages, it is explained as – to fall, to flow. Even here, if 'amavaiti' is considered to stand for 'courage',

1 Khordeh Avesta – Ardvi Sur Niyaesh – para – 4.

then the meaning of the hymn becomes absurd. 'Yao amavaiti fratachaiti' will become – which flows courageously. But rivers are nowhere described to be courageously flowing. The river of Vourukash i.e. Ardvi Sur was a mighty river. It flowed naturally. It is absurd to associate courage with natural flow of any river. 'Yao amavaiti fratachaiti' says – which flows through Amavart. Zoroastrians called their home land – Amavart or Amavant. We know that the river Aredvi Sur was none other than the river Narmada. In those grand old days, India was called – Amavart.

Let us look at it in another way. We have innumerable references of the twin words 'Haurvtat-Amvrvtat' throughout Zoroastrian religious texts. It is interesting to get into the meaning of these two words. In Zoroastrian mythology these are considered to be the names of two Bountiful Immortals. The other Bountiful Immortals are – Ahura, Vohu mana, Asha vahista, Xatra vairya, and Spenta armaiti. Zoroastrians believe that there are altogether seven Bountiful Immortals. Thus 'Haurvtat-Amvrvtat' are the names of Zoroastrian deities. They are proper nouns. But, at the same time, these words have also been attributed different meanings in translations of Avestan scriptures. 'Haurvtat' is explained to be 'wholeness' or 'perfection' and, at the same time, it is also considered to be the name of a female deity who is supposed to be ruling over waters. 'Amvarvtat' is explained as 'immortality' and, at the same time, it is also considered to be the name of the Holy Spirit that presides over 'immortality' and 'vegetation kingdom'.

Throughout Avestan texts 'Haurvtat-Amvarvtat' form an inseparable pair. They are always referred to and worshipped together. It is believed that, at times, one of them conveys the sense of vigour and endurance whereas the other refers to something like perfection and immortality. They are also considered to be an expression that draws parallels between earthly and heavenly virtues. We are told 'Haurvtat' figuratively represents ambrosia and 'Amvarvtat' is believed to represent nectar. Isn't all this quite confusing? Firstly, why should 'Haurvtat' be considered as the deity who presides over waters? We know that the Goddess of waters in Avestan mythology was 'Ardvi Sur'. 'Ardvi Sur Anahita' of Zoroastrian mythology became 'Ardvi Sur Nahid' in Old Persian. Since 'Nahid' is also the name of 'Venus', her first statue was erected by Antaxerxes (404 – 361 BC) under the name of Venus-Anahita. Thus she became the Anaitis of Greek mythology. But the most important thing to consider is – what leads them to sense that something earthly is compared and contrasted with a heavenly virtue. None of the meanings attributed to both words indicate in any fashion that Haurvtat-Amvarvtat could be compartmentalized as earthly and heavenly. Yet, the Zoroastrians could, some how, perceive that a parallel was drawn between something earthly and heavenly by the twin words – Haurvtat-Amvarvtat. Why? Could it be that the words have had some other meaning that changed with the passage of time?

Haurvtat could easily be considered as the Avestan transcription of 'Saurvtat'. In Zoroastrian scriptures, we find many examples where 's' is invariably replaced by 'h'. We know that 'Saur' is a Sanskrit word. It stands for – 'solar'. Now we do perceive of something heavenly. And if this heavenly thing is to be contrasted with something earthly then Amvarvtat has to refer to this earth. 'Amvarvtat' is 'Amavartat' which exactly means – in Amavart. In the days of Gatha, Amavart was the name of this country. Similarly, 'Haurvtat' or 'Saurvartat' can be translated as - 'in Saurvart'. 'Saurvart' literally stands for – the land of the Sun or the land of the rising Sun. Thus, 'Haurvtat-Amavartat' could definitely be – in Amavart, the land of the rising Sun. Now observe the following hymn of Zoroastrian Gatha –

xCaqrOi hOi haurwAtA amvarvtAtA[1]

Here 'q' is pronounced as't' or 'th'. The corresponding identical word of 'xCaqrOi' in Sanskrit is – 'kshatroi'. It is derived from the root word 'kshatra', which stands for land, nation or empire. The meaning of 'hOi' is – to be, is. Thus haurwAtA-amvarvtAtA has to be the name of this land or nation. It can never be things like perfection, vigour, immortality etc. This hymn of Yasna-45 can be translated exactly as –

This land is Amavart, the land of the rising Sun.

Observe another hymn of Avestan Gatha –

mazdA xCaqrvmcA haurwatAtO[2]

'xCaqrvm' (kshatravam) is empire, land, region. We know that 'mazdA xCaqrvm' stands for 'the region of mazda'. 'Mazda' is the corresponding identical of Sanskrit word – 'medha', which stands for 'brilliance' or 'bright rays'. Its place of existence is always associated with the abode of the Sun. The hymn can be translated exactly as –

The region of these bright rays is at 'haurwat' (saurvart).

How could 'haurvat' be ambrosia, perfection or wholeness? 'Haurwat' is the abode of the Sun. It is 'Haurvart'. It is the corresponding identical of 'Saurvart'.

'Haurwat' stands for – solar. Now observe the following line –

mazdi dadAT ahurO haurwatO amvarvtAtascA[3]

1 Gatha – Yasna – 45 – para – (10).
2 Gatha – Yasna – 34 – para – (1).
3 Gatha – Yasna – 31 – para – (21).

It says – 'Lord Ahura gave bright rays in this land of the rising Sun, which is Amavart.' It is interesting to note that this land 'Haurwart' i.e. 'Saurvart' was also called 'Vmawant' in Avestan religious texts. Observe the following line of Zoroastrian Gatha –

parStVm zI qBA YaqanA tat Vmawat&m[1]
hyaT qBA xCay&S aECvm dyAT VmawaNtvm

Each and every word of this hymn is identically found in Sanskrit as well. 'parStVm' stands for – 'giving birth'. Here the root word is – 'pras'. 'Qba' (pronounced as 'tva') is 'you' and 'YaqanA' can be translated as – 'where'. 'tat' stands for 'there'. 'Vmawat&m' is the country or the empire of the Sun. Here, the root word is 'Va' which means 'radiant' or 'shinning brightly'. In Sanskrit, the Sun is also called as 'Vanu' and 'Vashkar'. Similarly, 'Vma' or 'Vama' is 'the Sun' and 'wat' or 'wart' can be translated as – the land, country or empire. Thus, the first line of the hymn says –

Where you are born (each morning)
There exists the empire of the Sun.

'hyaT' is 'here' and 'xCay&S' is the corresponding identical of 'kshayah' of Sanskrit, which stands for – residence or dwelling place. 'aECvm' means 'such' and 'dyAT' is – the act of giving. The second line of the hymn proclaims –

Here lies your dwelling place
Such is the land of VmawaNt – given to us

This hymn of Gatha clearly establishes the fact that 'haurvart' exactly meant 'saurvart' i.e. the land or empire of the rising Sun. In Zoroastrian scriptures, this region of rising Sun was also called – 'Vamavant' or 'Vamavart'.

---

1 Gatha – Yasna – 43 – para – (10).

'Haurvatat' had become 'Hordad' in later Zoroastrian liturgical texts. In Avestan religious books the chapter 'Hordad Yasht' is consecrated to 'Haurvatat', where she is invoked as the protector of seasons and years. There we are! We know that seasons and years are manifestations of the Sun alone. They are directly related with the position of the Sun. It is only the Sun that causes change of seasons and years. 'Haurvat' is none other than 'Saurvart'. It pertains to the – 'solar world'. Now observe the following Avestan hymn -

Idha Haurvata Amertata[1]
yoi sto mizdem ashaunam
paro asti jasentam
mana dami Zarathushtra

In the religious texts of Parsees it is translated as – 'Here is self-realization and immortality which are the rewards of righteous when they go to the world beyond. O Zarathushtra, of wise mentality.' But the meaning of the third line is-absolutely clear. It says – 'away remains every kind of harm or wound'. Does it not indicate that the remaining lines pertain to something that happens here? Let us go through the meaning of each word -

Idha	-	here
Haurvata	-	the land or region of the Sun
AmertAta	-	in Amavart
Yoi	-	whosoever
Sto	-	worship
Mizdem	-	of Mazda
Ashaunam	-	deity
Paro	-	away
Asti	-	is
Jasentam	-	to cause harm, to wound

1 Khordeh Avesta – Hormazd Yasht – para – (25).

Man	-	thought, conviction
Dami	-	certainty
Zarathushtra	-	name of the Prophet

It says – 'Here in Haurvata-Amertata – whosoever worships Mazda, away remains from him every kind of harm or wound, take it for granted O Zarathushtra'. Haurvata-Amertata has to be the name of a place. It stands for – Amavart, the land of the rising Sun. Observe the following line of Meher Niyaesh of Khordeh Avesta –

Tem amavantem yazatem surem[1]

In Zoroastrian religious texts, the translation of the aforesaid line is given as – 'that courageous, most worthy of adoration'. Zoroastrian texts explain 'suram' as 'strong' and 'brave'. But this is, again, a misconception. Observe the following line of 'Ardibehesht Yasht; -

Surem Mazdadhatem Yazamaide[2]

How can 'surem' be 'strong' and 'brave' in this hymn? 'Mazdadhatem' is – the giver of Mazda. If we go by the suggested meaning of 'surem' then the meaning of the hymn becomes –

Strong and brave people worship the giver of Mazda

But, in those days, Lord Ahura was not worshipped only by men who were strong and brave. He was the giver of Mazda and he was worshipped by every one. 'Surem' can not be 'strong and brave'. Here, 'surem' stands for deities. The hymn describes that –

Even deities worship the Giver of Mazda (Lord Ahura)

The things become absolutely clear when we come across – 'yasnem Surem' in 'Havan Geh' of Khordeh Avesta'. Avestan

1 Khordeh Avesta – Meher Niyaesh – para – (15).

2 Khordeh Avesta – Ardibehesht Yasht – line (19).

'Yasna' is the corresponding identical of the word 'Yagya' of Sanskrit. We know that 'Havan' is performed during Yagya ceremonies and divinities are invoked. 'Yasnem Surem' exactly stands for – the deities of Yasna (Yagya). Strong and brave have got nothing to do with Yagya.

Since all words of the aforesaid line of Meher Niyaesh are found in Sanskrit language as well, let us consider the word-by-word meaning of the whole line –

Tem	-	him
amavantem	-	?
Yazatem	-	worship
Surem	-	deities

'Tem Yazatem Surem' is 'Divinities worship him'. Deities or divinities are generally not called courageous or strong. 'Amavant' can never mean something like 'courageous' or 'brave'. 'Courageous deities worship him' is an unusual statement that doesn't make sense. Therefore, 'Amavant' could not be strong or courageous. 'Amavant' is the name of some place. 'Amavantem' exactly means – of Amavant. The whole line can be translated as –

'Even the divinities of Amavant worship him'.

Now observe the following hymn of Yasna – 34 of Zoroastrian Gatha –

At tOi ubE haurwIscA XarvqAi A amvrvtaitIscA[1]

The word by word meaning can be given as –

At	–	here
tOi	–	you
ubE	–	arise, appear
haurwIs Ca	–	in the East

1 Gatha – Yasna – 34 – para – (11).

XarvqAi – to fall, to flow down
amvrvtaitIs Ca – in Amavart

The hymn is attributed to the bright rays of Lord Ahura i.e. the Sun God. The hymn describes that the bright rays of the Sun arise in the East and fall in the region of Amavart.

In pre-Aryan era, this country had an altogether different name. In those days, India was called – Amavant.

Zoroaster

NAismI daEwo[1]

These are believed to be the words of Zoroaster himself. The hymn says – I am no Daewa (God). Greatness and humility always go together. Zoroaster was not an ordinary man. He was the first Prophet. He was the earliest 'Chosen One' – to whom God revealed his scheme of creation. None had preceded him as the messenger of Almighty, who was sent to establish order and peace in this world full of pain and strife. He was to mouth the words of Ahura, in the language of convenience, so that love and harmony could be established in a decaying world. Later, God might have thought of repeating the exercise when, in the following millennia, he sent some more messengers on to this earth. To them also, he communicated directly, as he had done before. Even they have had revealed wisdom. Even they endeavoured to usher happiness in this world. Each one of them was considered the Blessed One. Each was a divine incarnation. Whatever they said was to develop into a distinct religion. Whatever they got inspired from was to become the symbolic design of the Almighty.

But very little is known about the first Prophet of this earth. Obscure is the place where he dwelt. Doubtful is the land where originated the Zoroastrian philosophy. Confusing is the meaning of the name – Zoroaster itself. Even the name of the Prophet was not Zoroaster. He was called Zarathushtra. Zoroaster is the Greek transliteration of the name Zarathushtra. Since ages, scholars have tried to explain the meaning of this name. Zarathushtra is a combination of

1 Gatha – Yasna – 12 – para – (1).

two words. It is a compound word. According to Parsee belief Zoroaster himself reared a herd of camels. One of his camels was 'Zaray' which is an Avestan word for 'yellow' or 'golden'. 'Ushtra' is the Avestan word for camel. Thus was called Zarathushtra, which implied 'the keeper of yellow camel' or 'the keeper of golden camel'. Some Zoroastrians have come forward with yet another explanation. They consider the root Avestan word to be 'Zarat' which means 'old'. According to them - Zarathushtra means 'the keeper of the old camels'. Some have yet another explanation. They say that the Avestan word 'Zara' is 'light' and 'Tusht' means 'friend' or 'lover'. Zarathushtra was named so because he was 'the one who loves the light'. Some say it is 'Zara ushas' which means 'golden light'. Another school of thought suggests that Zoroaster was 'the golden star '. Here the root words considered are 'Zaray' and 'Aster'.

The Oxford dictionary of Philosophy places Zoroaster at the first place in the chronology of Philosophers. Since last 2500 years, almost all philosophers of repute have been referring to his work, directly or indirectly.

Ancient Greek and Roman philosophy was greatly influenced by Zoroastrian faith. In Greece, the earliest mention of Zoroaster's name is found in the works of 'Xanthus' of Lydia. Xanthus was the contemporary of Herodotus and had lived in fifth century BC. Pliny mentioned about Zoroaster in 'Natural History' where it is said that he had laughed on the day of his birth. Voltaire believed that Zoroaster was the founder of rational deism. Rabindra Nath Tagore considered him as the one and only true Prophet that ever lived on this earth. Aristotle places the date of the Prophet somewhere around 9600 B.C. Oleg Petrov tells us that according to Zoroastrian traditions he flourished in 588 B.C. i.e. 258 years before Alexander conquered Persia.

But this 'traditional date' also had Greeko-Persian background. It originated immediately after Alexander's conquest of Persia. The Seleucid kings who had succeeded Alexander wanted to commemorate the conquest of Alexander by instituting a new calendar in Persia. This was not acceptable to the followers of Zoroaster who were inhabitants of Persia. They opposed the endeavours of Seleucid kings and tried to establish the era of Prophet Zoroaster so that they could start a new calendar of their own, which could be based on Zoroastrian era. They calculated the era of Zoroaster by counting the successive generations and came to the conclusion that Zoroaster must have lived two hundred and fifty-eight years before Alexander. Tradition also had that Zoroaster died at the age of 77. Thus, it was calculated that Zoroaster was born about 628 B.C. and died in 551 BC. For quite sometime, scholars all over world, believed in this 'Traditional date'. But in late nineteenth century people raised serious objections with this Traditional date. The most important difficulty was of linguist origin. The Old Avestan and Vedic Sanskrit are very similar and hence, cannot be separated by more than a few centuries. Based on above fact it was presumed that era of Zoroaster could be around 1000 BC. However, some of the western scholars place him much earlier and according to Mills, his era could be beyond 1500 B.C. Boyce believed that Zoroastrian era was any time in between 1700 to 1500 B.C. However, Archaeological findings of B-M-A-C (Bactria-Margiana-Archaeological-Complex) have refuted even these dates and pushed the Zoroastrian era further back to any time prior to 2200 BC. Pliny, who compared both Moses and Zoroaster, thought that Zoroaster lived several thousand years before Moses.

Ever since ancient Greek times Zoroaster has been considered as 'the mysterious Eastern Wisdom'. Zoroastrians believe that their Prophet was born some five thousand years ago at 'Raya' in Iran. Some have suggested that 'Aran' on the river 'Arexes', was the home land of Aryans and Zoroaster. This place is suggested to be close to the northwestern frontier of Media. Some say that he had his residence in 'Ragha'- another place in Iran. 'al-Shaharastani', who originated from Shahristan i.e. present day Turkmenistan, proposed that Zoroaster's father was from 'Atropatene' and his mother, was from 'Rai'. According to 'Gnoli' his original land was 'Sistan'. 'Sarianidi' proposed the B-M-A-C region and 'Boyce' suggested it could be the Steppes. By late twentieth century, consensus had settled on his origin in Eastern-Iran or Central Asia.

But it is important to note that nowhere in older Avestan texts we get any mention of places, rivers, mountains, tribes or kingdoms that could be identified as Central Asian or Iranian. On the other hand, we have fairly concluded that Narmada Valley was the home land of earliest Zoroastrians and their ancestors. Could it be that even Zoroaster was an Indian? Before we start a proper probe to ascertain the Zoroastrian land, let us see what Avestan Gatha has to say about the prophet Zoroaster, in particular, and the Aryans, in general. Observe the following lines of Avestan Gatha –

airyVmA iKyO rafvDrAi jaNtU[1]
nvrvbyascA nAiribyascA zaraquStrahE
WaMhVuS rafvDrAi manaMhO

Its word-by-word meaning is as follows-

AiryVmA - Aryans

IKyO - One

RafvDrAi - Doubtful, having perpetual doubts

1 Gatha – Yasna – 54 – para – (1).

JaNtU	-	Creatures
Nvrvbyasca	-	Men
NAiribyasca	-	Women
ZarathUStrahE	-	Zoroaster
WahMVuS	-	Invite
ManaMhO	-	mind

The whole thing can be translated as – 'Aryans are one such creatures that have perpetual doubts. Their men and women often invited Zoroaster to clarify the doubts of their mind.' These lines clearly pronounce that Zoroaster and Aryans coexisted harmoniously. But where did it happen? Was it Iran? Did Aryans and Zoroaster live together, in fourth or fifth millennium B. C., in Iran? Or was it some other country? According to some scholars the oldest Avestan texts originated among the ancient Aryans who inhabited the area between the Aral Sea and modern Afghanistan i.e. in the area of modern Turkmenistan, Uzbekistan and Tajikistan. Could it be that Aryans and Zoroaster lived together in one of these countries? Had there not been any other reference in the Avestan texts, the endeavour to locate exactly this land of Aryans and Zoroaster would have been extremely difficult. But it is there. It is all there in the Gatha. In Yasna 31 Zoroaster himself says –

maibyO xCaqrvm aojONghwaT[1]

'Maibyo' is the Avestan as well as, the Sanskrit word for 'my' or 'mine'. 'XCathrvm' is the corresponding equivalent of Sanskrit – 'kshatram'- and in both languages; it stands for 'place', 'area' or 'land'. Thus, the whole thing can be translated as – 'I belong to (my place is) aojONghwat'. 'aojONghwat' is certainly the name of a place - the place to which Zoroaster belonged.

1 Gatha – Yasna – 31 – para – (4).

But even after this disclosure we remain as clueless as ever. We do not have the slightest idea of 'aojONghwat'. Later Zoroastrian scriptures are absolutely silent on this subject. It is strange. There has to be some reason for this.

Modern languages evolve to take place of the old ones. It is a gradual process of transformation of means of expression. It is never a sudden phenomenon. The new language also inherits all ideas and information of the old ones. Transformation of languages and ideas are two mutually exclusive events that seldom coincide. It is not that when Old Persian replaced Avesta, the natives of Iran stopped discussing their religion. 'aojONghwat' was still the birthplace of their Prophet. Its proper mention in Old Persian liturgical texts was so inevitable. But it is not there. It is unnatural to presume that, when Avesta gave way to Old Persian, people suddenly changed their Zoroastrian way of living. They could not. They had no alternative. Persian speaking Iranians were equally Zoroastrian. How could their religious texts not contain this specific information about place of birth of their own Prophet? What was 'aojONghwat' called in Persian? Where was born the Prophet of Pahlavi or Pazend or Persian speaking Iranians? This lack of information is significant. It confirms that, even in those days, 'aojONghwat' was not understood. It confirms that Old Persian speaking people were not familiar with this place of birth. It confirms that they did not understand the Avestan language. Neither could they identify any of the places related with Zoroaster's life. It further confirms that both Zoroaster and Avesta belonged to a different geographical terrain, with which Old Persian or Pahlavi speaking Zoroastrians were not familiar.

Thousands of years have gone by, since Zoroaster's era. Most of the related things are extinct. It is absolutely difficult to reconstruct the true story of development of a philosophy, which is more than five thousand years old. The few facts that we have, are neither enough nor conclusive. Yet, we will try to arrange things, as properly as we can, so that we have a faint glimpse of the evolution of a religion. It is a fairly concluded fact that the forefathers of ancient Aryans of Iran were original inhabitants of Narmada Valley. Could it be that even 'aojONghwat' was a place somewhere in India? But it is impossible to proceed any further. 'aojONghwat' just doesn't make sense. Apparently, it doesn't even seem to be the name of a place. We know that phonetic transcriptions of Avestan words were, at places, not carried out in strict sequence of pronunciation. We frequently come across places in Zoroastrian scriptures where 'gao-O' is written as 'aog-O' and 'sarv-vikhyat' written as 'varvS-vikhyat'. 'aojONghwat' also might be containing, in its present design, some similar aberration. But it is difficult to ascertain that. There is no way to pin point the error. The solution has to be there in the Avestan religious texts alone. In Yasna 34, we again come across the mention of this place. But here, the name is expressed somewhat differently. Here it is mentioned as – 'aojOMhwaNtvm'. We know – it is the same place. But it remains equally incomprehensible here too. We cannot correlate 'aojOMhwaNtvm' with any place that exists in this world today. We need some more information about this 'aojOMhwaNtvm' or 'aojONghwat'. In Yasna 28, we again come across the mention of this place. But here, the name is expressed somewhat differently. Observe the line –

xCaqrvmcA aGZaonwamnvm[1]

Here, again, we are talking about the same place. It is an established fact that 'aGZaonwamnvm' is certainly the name of some place. The context is self-explanatory. No other meaning can be attributed to it. 'xCaqrvam' is the Avestan inscription

1 Gatha – Yasna – 28 – para – (3).

of the word 'kshatravam'. It stands for area or land. It says that the name of that place is 'aGZaonwamnvm'. But here the name has been spelt in somewhat different manner. At last, it does sound some sense here. 'gazao' or 'gajao' is something familiar. We know that it is a proper Sanskrit word. It is the Sanskrit word for elephant. 'gajao' (gaj) and 'hasti' are synonyms and both these words have been in general use since ancient days. We have many places in India, which start either with 'gaj' or with 'hasti'. In fact, 'Hastinapur' was one of the most important kingdoms of ancient India. Hey! There we are! We have got it! 'Gajaowhat' was the ancient name of 'Hastinapur' itself. This 'aojONghwat'/GZaonwamnvm is 'GZaojonghwat'. It is our 'Hastinapur'. We need not rearrange 'aojONghwat'. It has been straightened out to its comprehensible form in the Gatha itself. This Avestan 'aojONghwat' is 'Gajaonghwhat' only. Incorporation of nasal sound is the peculiar characteristic of Avestan language. With incorporation of nasal sound the other name of 'Hastinapur' i.e. 'Gajaowhat' becomes 'Gajaonghwat'. Thus, strictly according to Avestan texts – Zoroaster was born at Hastinapur. 'MaibyO xCathrvm aojONghwat' reveals that Zoroaster hailed from Gajaowhat.

Let us come to the other important place that is related with the life of Zoroaster. Followers of Zoroaster believe that their Prophet got enlightened on the mountains of 'Ushideren'. This is again a misconception. There is no place in or around Iran which can be identified with Ushideren. In Avestan Gatha, this place is written as 'uCidarvanam'. It is pronounced as 'Ushidarvanam'. It is a compound word. It is made up of two words – 'Ushi' and 'Darvanam'. 'Usha' or 'Ushi' is the Goddess of Dawn. 'Darvanam' is derived from the root word 'Driv', which exactly means - resting place. Together the mixed expression 'Ushidarvanam' stands for – 'the resting place of the Goddess of Dawn'. Zoroastrian religious texts also proclaim that Ushideren was also the abode of Ahura. In Avestan texts, the Sun is considered as the true physical manifestation of Lord Ahura. Since Ahura was the Sun God, it was very natural to associate his abode along with the resting place of Usha – the Goddess of Dawn. One can easily perceive why Ushideren was also considered as the abode of Lord Ahura. Each morning Usha descends on to this earth from the Eastern horizon. Every morning she brings her ethereal light feathered radiance, which is so pleasing to the senses. 'Usha' always comes, clad in her snowy white apparel, from the East. And she is always followed by the most powerful of all the heavenly bodies – the Sun. Avestan word – 'Verethraghna' means slayer of darkness. In Avestan scriptures, it is a commonly used epithet of Ahura. Thus, Ahura is none other than the Sun God and his abode is reasonably associated, in Zoroastrian hymns, with the resting place of Usha. In Vedic mythology too, Usha – the Goddess of Dawn - is always described to be associated with the Sun. Observe the following lines of Atharva Veda –

'Ever as a lover followeth a maiden[1]
so doth the Sun the Dawn'

Similarly, Rig-Veda – Mandala 1 – Hymn 115 describes that the Sun follows the Goddess of Dawn (Usha) exactly as men follow women. Since the Sun immediately follows her footsteps and rises from the same part of the horizon, it was appropriate on the part of the early Zoroastrians to assign him the same abode where Usha rests in the night. 'Ushidarvanam' was definitely the abode of Ahura. It could not be the name of any place located on this earth. But I do not know how this resting place of Goddess of Dawn was further declared as the seat of enlightenment of the Prophet. We have the mention of Zoroaster's enlightenment in the Gathas. And we have the

1 Atharva Veda – Hymn – (107).

name of that particular place too, where he got enlightened. It is certainly not Ushideren.

The Avestan line goes as –

Y&M daEn&m ahurO saoKyantO dadAt[1]

'Y&M' (yam) is a word that is identically found in Avesta and Sanskrit. It stands for – this. 'Daenam' is religion. 'Saokyanto' means – at Saokyant. 'Dadat' can be translated as – gave. Here the root word is – Da. In both languages 'Da' is – to give. Thus the whole line can be translated as –

This religion was given (revealed) by Ahura at Saokyant.

This Saokyant had to be one of the most sacred places of Zoroastrians. It must have been the place of enlightenment of Zoroaster. It was here that the sacred religious philosophy was revealed to Zoroaster – by Lord Ahura. But we get stuck at this point. Where could it be? We do not have any idea about this place – which was called Saokyant in those ancient days. How do we proceed now? We need further clues about Saokyant. And it has to come from Avestan hymns alone. In this regard, there is another similar hymn that gives out the name of the place where Zoroaster got enlightened. Observe the following hymn of Khordeh Avesta –

Yao hacha Gayat marethnat A saoshyantat verethraghnat[2]

First of all, let us analyse the meaning of the first half of the hymn. In both languages, 'Yao' stands for – who. 'Gayat' can be translated as – at the place called Gaya. In both Avesta and Sanskrit, 'Marethnat' means – died. Thus, the first half of the hymn can be translated as –

Who died at Gaya

---

1 Gatha – Yasna – 53 – para – (2).

2 Khordeh Avesta – Prayer for Rembering the Dead – Para – (9).

This hymn refers to the place where Zoroaster had breathed his last. This fact is also corroborated by the following hymn of Yasna – 51 of Zoroastrian Gatha –

Mazdi dAtA mraoT gayehyE[1]

'Mazdi data' is the giver of Mazdayasni religion (Zoroaster). 'Mraot Gayehye' can be translated as – died at Gaya. This hymn, again, gives out the exact place where the Prophet Zoroaster had breathed his last. It was – Gaya. Isn't that Strange? Isn't it the same place where Lord Buddha got enlightened? If we are anywhere near truth then, from now on, this place is going to be considered as – thrice holy city. Firstly, it is the holiest place of Hindus. The religious rites called 'Pind-daan' are performed at this place. Followers of Hinduism believe that the rites of 'Pind-daan' are essential for salvation of souls of the departed ones. Since time immemorial, Indians come to Gaya from every nook and corner, to perform this religious rite - for salvation of the souls of their deceased near and dear ones. Secondly, Gaya is the place of pilgrimage for Buddhists too. It was here, on the banks of river Niranjana, that Lord Buddha got enlightened. Buddhists from all over world come to Gaya to worship this place of enlightenment. And from now on – this place is going to be the most sacred place for Zoroastrians as well. Gaya was the place where the first Prophet of this world – Zoroaster – had breathed his last. From now on – Gaya is going to be the most important centre of pilgrimage for the followers of Mazdayasni religion as well. According to these hymns of Avestan Gatha – Zoroaster died at Gaya.

And now we come to the remaining part of the aforesaid hymn of prayer for the dead. We have seen earlier that 'Yao hacha Gayat marethnat' revealed that Zoroaster had died

1 Gatha – Yasna – 51 – para – (19).

at Gaya. Now let us analyse the second half of the hymn. 'A', here, denotes the sense of – and. 'Saoshyantat' can be translated as – at Saoshyant. 'Verethraghnat' is a compound word. It is made up of 'Verethra', which is – darkness. It is the corresponding identical of Sanskrit word – Vritra. Similarly, 'Ghna' is identically present in both languages. It can be translated as – to kill. Thus, 'Verethraghnat' means – killing or removal of darkness. In Avestan texts, 'Verethraghna' is also used as an epithet of Ahura – the Sun God – because, every morning, the Sun removes or kills darkness and spreads light all around. Even here, 'Verethraghnat' conveys the same sense. Therefore, the remaining half of the hymn (A saoshyantat verethraghnat) can be translated as –

And whose darkness was killed at Saoshyant

It was Saoshyant where Zoroaster got enlightened. At Saoshyant his darkness i.e. ignorance got killed or removed. Thus, the complete hymn – 'Yao hacha Gayat marethnat A saoshyantat verethraghnat' can be translated as –

Who died at Gaya and who got enlightened at Saoshyant

But before we proceed further, we come across a genuine problem. In Avestan scriptures – Saoshyant has been assigned a very important and interesting meaning. In Zoroastrian religious texts 'SaoshyaNt' is considered as something close to 'useful' or 'profitable' or 'savior' or 'helper'. It is also the name given to the Order of Being, who shall appear in this world, to fight the evil and re-establish the Law of righteousness. However, this can not be the true meaning of the word – Saoshyant. I am of the opinion that Saoshyant is the erroneous transcription of the word – Saokyant. We have seen earlier that Saokyant was the place where the religion was revealed by Ahura. Therefore, the place of enlightenment of Zoroaster was – Saokyant. It was at Saokyant that his ignorance was killed.

Saoshyant had to be the erronneus transcription of Saokyant only. And we are not wrong. 'Yao hacha Gayat marethnat A saoshyantat verethraghnat' is the hymn taken from Yasna – 59 of Gatha. Observe what the hymn of Yasna – 59 says –

YI haca gayAT marvqnaT A saoKyaNtAt WvrvqraGnaT[1]

Therefore, we may now conclude that Saoshyant is the erroneous transcription of Saokyant and that Zoroaster got enlightened at the place called Saokyant. We have another very interesting hymn on this subject. Observe the following hymn of 'Sarosh Yasht Hadokht' of Khordeh Avesta –

Hakhaya ahmakem Saoshyantam yat bipaitishtanam acaonam[2]

We have seen earlier that, in Avesta; 'prati' is invariably written as – 'paiti'. The Avestan word 'bipaitishtanam' is the corresponding identical of the Sanskrit word – 'bipratishthanam'. This 'bipaitishtanam' or 'bipratishthanam' can be translated as – to become famous. 'Yat' stands for – where. It is the corresponding identical of Sanskrit – Yatra. 'Acaonam' refers to Zoroaster. 'Yat bipaitishtanam acaonam' can be translated as –

Where Zoroaster became famous

Observe that 'yat' is the key word here. 'Where Zoroaster became famous' - remains an incomplete expression. It requires mention of name of some place – where Zoroaster became famous. And it is there in the hymn. 'Hakhaya ahmakem Saoshyantam' is – beloved is my place Saokyantam. We know that Saoshyantam is the erronneus transcription of Saokyantam. Avestan 'Hakhaya' is the corresponding identical of Sanskrit – Sakhaya. It stands for – loved ones, friends. 'Ahmakem' means – my or mine.Thus, the whole hymn can be translated as –

1 Gatha – Yasna – 59 – para – (27).

2 Khordeh Avesta – Sarosh Yasht Hadokht – para – (16).

Beloved is our place Saokyantam where the
Prophet became famous.

It was at Saokyantam where Zoroaster got enlightened. It was at Saokyantam where he became famous. This place was loved and worshipped by ancient Zoroastrians. But where could this Saokyantam be? About this – I have a very strong feeling. I strongly feel that even this place – like Gaya – has to have some kind of relation to Buddhist mythology. We know that Lord Buddha died at Kasya. This is the name of the exact place where Buddha died. It is in Kushinagar district of Uttar Pradesh. Could it be that this place – Saokyantam – is 'Kasya' itself? 'Antam' is a word found identically in Avesta as well as in Sanskrit. It stands for – end or limit. In both languages it is also used as a suffix – conveying similar meaning. 'Vanantam' of Sanskrit and 'Vanaintim' of Avesta are just the same. 'Van' is forest and 'Vanantam' exactly means – the end or the limit or boundary of forest. I feel that the suffix 'antam' is there in Saokyantam as well. In that case – the meaning of Saokyantam will become – at the boundary or periphery of Saoky. Could it be that 'Saoky' is the erroneous transcription of – 'ksyao' (Kasya). Avestan texts are full of such aberrations. We have observed earlier how 'sarv-vikhyat' has been erroneously transcribed as 'vrvS-vikhyat' in Avestan scriptures. Similarly, in Yasna – 10 of Zoroastrian Gatha, we notice that the word 'gairim' is transcribed as – zAirim. Another example is 'nAismI daEwO' which is, at another place, erroneously transcribed as – rAismI daEwO. I can not say much about it. But we have another interesting hymn on this subject. It says –

prVNdIm Y&m ca bipaitiStan&m aCaonIm[1]

It says – Prvndim is the place where the Prophet became famous.

1 Gatha – Yasna – 13 – para – (1).

Here we have the mention of another place 'prvndim' – where Zoroaster is believed to have got enlightened and become famous. But here the name of the place is given without any prefix or suffix attached to it. This 'prvndim' is easy to rearrange to provide some meaning. There is just one vowel and very limited choices of recombination exist. It is simply 'pdrvnim' i.e. Padrvna which is 'Padraona' these days. There we are! In all probability, Zoroastrians knew that it was Padraona where the Prophet got enlightened. This Padraona was situated at 'Kasyaontm' i.e. on the outer limits of Kasya – just twenty kilo metres away from Kasya.

Therefore, we may conclude that Zoroaster was born at Hastinapur, died at the place called Gaya, and in all probability, he got enlightened at Padraona, which is in Kushinagar district. Isn't that strange? It is certain now that Zoroaster had died at Gaya. Almost three thousand years after that incident, Gaya was to become the seat of enlightenment of Lord Buddha. Zoroaster, in all probability, got enlightened at Kushinagar. Roughly three thousand years later, Kushinagar was to become the place of Mahaparinibban (death) of Buddha. Isn't this bewildering? My God! What am I to say?

ZOROASTER'S RELIGION

Vishp humata Vishp hukhta Vishp hvarshta baodhovarshta[1]

Zoroaster was the first to explain what is good. According to him, every thing that was benevolent to world was good. All thoughts, all speech, all actions that were benevolent to mankind were to be considered good. The hymn declares to the world - his definition of morality. It says –

Good thoughts, good speech and good action are to be considered as Baodh or Buddhist religious acts.

This was the first instance in this world where morality was wedded to religion. It took quite sometime for people to understand his design and almost more than thousands of years were to elapse before we could notice similar thoughts appear in other civilizations of this world. But good and bad has to always co-exist. Therefore Zoroaster also defined what is bad. He declared that all thoughts, all speech and all actions that are malevolent to world are bad and hence, they are considered not in accordance with Baodh or Buddhist religious acts.

Vishp dushmata Vishp duzukhta Vishp duzvarshta noit baodhovarshta[2]

It was the begining of Deism. Distinctly pronounced good or religious acts were contrasted with bad or irreligious deeds and humanity was advised to always stick to the former. However, the Prophet was aware of the frailties of human consciousness. He knew that the greed and easy virtue of human beings often tempted them to undertake immoral acts.

1 Khordeh Avesta – Vispa Humata.

2 Khordeh Avesta – Visp Humata.

Therefore, he put forth the concept of Spenta Mainyu i.e. the Good Spirit and Anaghra Mainyu or the Evil Spirit. He thought that an incessant fight between the Good and the Evil Spirit goes on within every individual and that the outcome of the war is clearly visible in the resultant action that is undertaken by the individual. If he succeeds in consciously eradicating the Evil Spirit from within, he tends to embark on the path of religion. If he succumbs to the allurements of Evil Spirit, he treads the path of irreligion. And this segregation of acts into two distinct compartments necessitated the idea of reward and punishment. Men would lead the life of virtue only if they are convinced of its benefits. Similarly, they would refrain from doing irreligious acts only if they knew that its consequences would certainly be unpleasant. But all rewards and punishments, which could be experienced in this world, were of material nature and it was not always possible, on the part of human beings, to realize the reward of a benevolent act, if it did not result in some material gain. Therefore, Zoroaster explained the concept of metaphysical worlds of 'heaven' and 'hell'. The idea of existence of heaven - with all its pleasing and beautiful attributes - was declared as the ultimate reward that awaited every virtuous soul. Similarly, existence of hell was portrayed - with all its miseries, pains and unpleasant things - as the future that was in store for all evildoers. This ultimate reward and punishment was of metaphysical nature and, with which, no material pleasures or pains could be equated. Heaven transcended all worldly pleasures. Each man's life after death was destined either for heaven or hell and it was the proper evaluation of the sum-total of all his activities on this earth that determined what he deserved. This evaluation was done by none other than the Almighty himself. Each was adjudged according to the acts he had performed in this world. Each was to serve the sentence in the next world. The Day of Judgment awaited every one. Thus was established the supremacy of the Almighty - Ahura. He reigned above all. He was the supreme arbitrator. He knew all that men thought, spoke or did. He was all knowing. He was ubiquitous. He was omnipotent. This is how the supreme God was understood in Zoroastrian religion.

The complex, yet harmonious design of this beautiful universe was attributed to Almighty – Ahur Mazda and his six 'Bountiful Immortals' or 'Ameshaspentas'. According to Zoroastrian mythology this world is governed by seven distinguished Ameshaspentas where each one looks after a distinct and important domain of natural phenomena. Since Ahur Mazda is the supreme authority that created all animate and inanimate things; the creation of these six Ameshaspentas is also attributed to him. The religion of Zoroaster also grants space for existence of some lesser deities or angels of comparatively subordinate stature who were called – 'Yazats'. The literal meaning of Yazat is 'Worthy of adoration'. It is derived from the root word 'Yaz' which stands for worship. These Yazats were believed to be the assistants of Ameshaspentas and, as such, they were grouped according to the Ameshaspenta to whom their cooperation was related. It is interesting to note that the Zoroastrian month has thirty days and that each day of the month is named after these seven Ameshaspentas and their assistant Yazats.

In Zoroastrian religion 'fire' was considered to be the most significant worldly manifestation of the Almighty himself. Gathic texts describe 'Athro' i.e. 'fire' as the son of Ahur Mazda. As such, it was considered to be the most sacred thing of this world. Worship of fire is the distinct characteristic feature of the followers of this Mazdayasni religion. The flame of fire is always erect and rising upwards. It does not get contaminated by worldly things and yet, contains the ability to purify everything. It was considered to be the most suitable vehicle for transporting worldly things to divinities. During religious ceremonies, Haoma (Soma) and other things of oblation were poured into the flames with a belief that fire was capable of transporting those offerings to heavenly deities. Fire was generally preserved in such ways that it could never get extinguished. This Eternal Flame was worshipped not only by Zoroastrians. 'Fire-cult' was the characteristic feature of ancient Aryan world too.

Worship of 'flame' is the most essential religious practice of the followers of Zoroastar. Even the establishment and consecration of these flames involve elaborate and well-defined rituals. Different kinds of 'fire' or 'flame' are accorded different degree of superiority. The holiest fire is called – 'Atash-Behram'. The other types of sacred fire are 'Adaran' and 'Dadgah'. Since the establishment and consecration of Adaran and Dadgah involves comparatively less tedious process, they are accorded second and third place in hierarchy of sacredness. Establishment of Adaran involves gathering of fire from the four classes of Zoroastrian society. Fire is gathered from the house of an Athornan, a Ratheshtran, a Vastaryoshin and a Hutokshan. All these fires undergo rituals of purification and are amalgamated. The consecration ceremony of an Adaran requires about eight priests and the whole process of establishment takes about two to three weeks. The consecrated flames of Adaran, like the holiest flame of Atash-Behram, are required to be kept burning forever. Dadgah is the lowest grade of fire. The ceremony involved in its establishment is much simpler. Only two priests are required to perform the consecration ceremony of the fire of a Dadgah.

But Atash-Behram is the most sacred fire. There are all together eight Atash-Behrams in whole of India. Four of them are established in Mumbai whereas two Atash-Behrams are established at Surat. The remaining two are located at Navsari and Udvada. The Atash-Behram of Udvada is the oldest. It is interesting to observe the complex and tedious process of establishment of the most sacred fire – Atash-Behram. It requires about thirty-two priests to complete the ceremony that generally takes about a year. It involves gathering of sixteen different kinds of fire. One of the sixteen distinct types is the lightning fire, which is quite difficult to obtain. It also involves collection of fire from those different trades in which furnace is used. But the most important thing to observe is that it also requires collection of fire from a cremation pyre. Isn't that bewildering? Zoroastrians are people who do not practice cremation. They have an altogether different, elaborate and complex process for disposal of dead bodies. They do not dispose off a dead body by burning. Burning of the dead is the distinguishing feature of Hinduism alone. Thus, we may conclude that each time an Atash-Behram is established, it necessitates inter-mixing of ritualistic elements from the two earliest religions of this world. Each time a flame is collected from the cremation pyre for amalgamation with the remaining fifteen varieties of fire; Hinduism and Zoroastrianism come closer. It is, indeed, a significant aspect of Zoroastrian traditions. I salute the wisdom of our ancestors who promoted such rituals. I wish there could have been, in all existing religions of this world, more such rituals that required inter-mixing of elements from different groups. It would have resulted into peaceful co-existence of followers of different faiths. It would have generated love and reverence for other faiths. Religious wars, crusades for prositylization and jihad could have, long back, ceased to exist.

However, let us now analyze some of the misconceptions that still prevail in both these earliest civilizations of world. 'Ahura' is the most important deity of Zoroastrian faith. But it is often erroneously explained as the corresponding identical of 'Asura' of Vedic Sanskrit. Asura in Sanskrit is – demon, therefore it is opined by some people that Zoroastrianism was the religion of Demon worship. Since Vedic 'soma' becomes 'haoma' in Avestan language and Vedic 'sakhya' becomes Avestan 'hakhya', historians were mislead in believing that Avestan 'Ahura' could be Vedic 'Asura'. Although Vedic's' is generally pronounced as 'h' in Avestan language, yet we come across many examples where Vedic and Avestan 's' is written and pronounced exactly as 's'. 'Sanghem', 'Saredha','Satem','Starem','Staomi', 'Saoka' and 'Shevist' are examples where 's' is written and pronounced exactly similarly in both languages. 'Suram' is another such word. It is there in both languages, with exactly similar pronunciation. The antonym of 'Suram' is 'Asuram' and therefore, it should exist in both languages exactly as it is – 'Asura'. There is no reason for assuming that 'Ahura' could be phonetic adaptation of 'Asura'. Since 'suram' does not become 'huram' in Avesta, there is no reason to suppose that its antonym 'asuram' would become 'ahuram'. Ahura worship could never be Asura worship i.e. 'cult of demon worship'.

But now we come to its more ridiculous part. 'Daeva' is the Sanskrit word for – Divinities. But, in Zoroastrian world, this word is explained as – Demon. Even they believe that the cult of Daeva worship of Vedic civilization was in fact – a cult of Demon worship. Zoroastrian religious texts reveal their faith to be – anti-Daevic. They believe that Mazdayasni was the religion given against Daevas i.e. Demons. I wonder what could lead them to have such conviction. 'Nemo Mithrai' is an Avestan line. It says – salutations to Mithra. 'Mitra' is invoked and worshipped throughout older as well as younger Avestan texts. Is he not one of the most important Vedic Daeva? Even 'Usha' – 'the Goddess of Dawn' – is worshipped in Mazdayasni religion. She is again, a Vedic Goddess. Observe the following Avestan line –

Usham sriram yazamaide

In Zoroastrian religious texts, it is translated as – 'we revere the beautiful Usha'.

'Apam-Naptarm', Haoma (Soma), Apo, Gawo (Cow), Athro (Agni), Aryamma, Ashva, Yam, Aoshadhi (Bheshaj) – these are all Vedic divinities i.e. Daevas. And all of these are worshipped in Avestan mythology as well. The Avestan line 'Apam Naptarem yazamaide' is 'we, hereby, revere Apam Naptarem'. Similarly, 'Nemo Geush' of Avesta is 'homage to cow'. It will be irrational to presume that Zoroastrianism was opposed to Daeva-cult. Even 'Vishwedeva' – an expression for collective body of all Daevas of world – is also revered in Gathic Hymns. How can such a religion be anti-Daevic? Zoroastrianism, from the very beginning, was not anti-Daevic. And neither was Daeva worship a cult of Demon worship. Observe the following hymn of Sarosh Yasht –

Ho noit tarshto franamaite[1]
Thwaeshat paro daevaebyo
Fra ahmat paro vispe daeva
Anusho tarshta nemente
Tarshta temangho dvarante

In Zoroastrian religious books it is translated as – 'he is not afraid or bows out of fear before the evil persons, on the contrary, all the evil persons, against their will, bow out of fear and out of fear run into darkness'.

However, this can not be the true meaning of the aforesaid hymns. Let us analyze the meaning of each word of these hymns. The same passage, when observed in Yasna 57 of Zoroastrian Gatha, reveals things somewhat different. There we find the word 'tvmaMhO' in the place of 'temangho'.

---

1 Khordeh Avesta – Sarosh Yasht Hadokht - para – (13).

'Temangho' is Avestan as well as Sanskrit word for – 'darkness'. But 'tvmaMhO' is a word derived from – 'tvam' i.e. 'you'. Since Gatha is the oldest scripture, we will consider 'tvmaMhO' to be the correct transcription.

In this hymn, 'tarshto' is the only word that needs clearification. In Zoroastrian religious books 'tarshto' is explained to stand for – afraid. But it does not make sense. In previous chapters we have read about the story of invention of 'Vajra' or 'thunder. Vedic as well as Avestan hymns attribute this invention to 'Taksha' i.e. 'Twashtra'. Here also, 'tarshto' is none other than 'Twashtra. The word 'anusho' is there in Vedic Sanskrit as well, where it stands for – afterwards. Similarly, 'nemente' is found in both languges. In both Avesta and Sanskrit, it is – act of worship, reverence. Thus 'anusho tarshta nemente' can be translated as – worship Tarshta afterwards. 'tarshto' could not be – afraid. It does not convey any thing meaningful. 'worship afraid afterwards' is meaningless. 'tarshta' is the name of a deity. In Vedic theology, Twashtra is believed to be the divinity who designes and makes every thing in this world. He is the divine engineer. The tradition has it that Twashtra is always worshipped before any other God. This Avestan 'tarshta' is the corresponding identical of Vedic 'Twashtra'. The hymn conveys the same belief. Observe the meaning of each word of this hymn-

Ho	–	who
Noit	–	not
Tarshto	–	God Twashtra
Franamaite	–	worship or salute
Twaeshat	–	jealously
Paro	–	away
Daevaebyo	–	Daevas

Fra – first, in the beginning

Ahmat – me

Vispe daeva – all Daevas of world

Anusho – afterwards

Nemente – salute or worship

TwmAmhO – you, yourself

Dvarante – to keep away, to drive away

'Ho noit tarshto franamaite' is – 'In case you do not (if you do not) worship or salute Twashtra'. 'Thwaeshat paro daevaebyo' can be translated as – 'and if you jealously keep away Daevas i.e. divinities'. ('Thwaeshat' is corresponding identical of – 'dwesh' of Sanskrit.) 'Fra ahmat paro vispe Daeva' is - 'if you keep me at the first place or salute me at the first place but keep all other Gods away with disregard'. 'anusho tarshto nemente' can be translated as – and if you worship Twashtra afterwards (or in the end).The meaning of the remaining part is absolutely clear. 'tarshta twmAmhO dvarante' is - then God Twarshta will drive you away. Things are absolutely clear. The religion of Zoroaster was not anti-Daevic. Even in Rig-Veda, we find almost similar practice of worshipping this divine engineer in the beginning of any religious ceremony. Observe the following line of Rig-Veda –

Ih Twashtaram Agriyam[1]

It says - we revere Twashtra at the first place. Twashtra was the engineer of Vedic divinities. The religion of Zoroaster was never anti-Daeva.

'Daevanam-Masyanam' is one of those paired expressions that are found innumerable times in Gatha and in later Avestan texts. We have its corresponding identical in Vedas as well.

1 Rig Veda – 1 – 13 – (132).

In Vedic texts also, we come across the paired expression of 'Daevam-Martyam'. In Sanskrit, it literally means – immortals as well as mortals. 'Daeva' in Sanskrit is God or Divinities, who are believed to be beyond the cycle of life and death. They are immortals. In this combined expression, they are compared with 'Martyas' i.e. those who face the reality of death. 'Martya', literally, can be translated as 'mortals' i.e. human being In Avestan texts also 'Masyanam' is explained as 'mortals' i.e. 'mankind'. If we take 'Daevanam' to be – Demons then 'Daevanam- Masyanam' of Avesta becomes – Demons and mortals. Now isn't that absurd? 'Immortals as well as mortals' or 'Divinity as well as mankind' is the right, sensible and frequently used expression found in almost all liturgical texts of this world. But 'Demons and humanity' is a meaningless, rare and unnatural expression. It almost corroborates our conclusion that 'Daevanam' of Avestan texts and Vedic Sanskrit was no different. In both languages it stood for divinity. In Holy Scriptures of Avesta, Zoroaster himself proclaims – 'Naesmi Daevo'. 'Naesmi' is a compound word made up of two components – 'Na' and 'Asmi'. 'Na Asmi' is identically found in Sanskrit as well and its meaning in both languages can be given as – 'I am not'. If 'Daevo' is translated as 'Demon' then the meaning of the Avestan line becomes – 'I am not a Demon'. Isn't that weired? How could the Prophet declare to the world that he was not a demon? He was the greatest religious teacher of his era and people often invited him for clarification of religious and philosophical doubts of their mind. There was absolutely no reason for proclaiming that he was not a demon. It again proves that 'Daevanam' of Avestan Hymns could never mean – Demon. Its true sense must have been exactly identical to 'Daeva' of Vedic Sanskrit. Now, the proclamation of Zoroaster does make sense. He was the religious guide of highest repute. His name and fame had reached far and wide. People had started considering him as some divine incarnation. But wisdom of Prophet refrained to accept it. He had to proclaim, time and again, that he was no God. Greatness and humility are complimentary. They often go together. When he declared to the world - 'Naesmi Daevo', he wanted them to believe that he was not any God or Divinity; he was simply one of them. The exact meaning of the Avestan word 'Daeva' becomes absolutely clear when we observe the following hymn –

daEwAiS cA xrafstrAiS makyAiS cA[1]

This hymn of Yasna – 19 clearly refers to all three orders of being. Here, 'daEwAis' is mentioned at the first place. Of the three, it is the most important. It refers to Gods or Divinities. 'xrafstrAiS' is mentioned after Daeva. It is pronounced as – kshrapstrais. The root word here is – 'kshah'. It is identically found in Sanskrit as well. 'Kshah' stands for – Demons. In fact the Sanskrit word 'kshapatah' exactly means Demons or Rakshasha. The third term – 'makyAiS', as usual, refers to mankind or mortals. This Avestan description of Gods, Demons and Mortals is corresponding identical of Daeva, Danava (asura) and mankind of Vedic texts. Avestan Daeva certainly meant Gods. It was no different from Vedic Daeva. Now, observe the following lines of Yasna – 52 of Avestan Gatha –

daEwan&m maKyAn&mCa[2]
arvKyaNt&m ahmAiCa nmAnAi

'daEwan&m maKyAn&mCa' can be translated as – Daevas (deities) and men. The root word in 'arvKyaNt&m' is 'arvak' which is identically found in Sanskrit as well, where it stands for – 'previously'. 'ahmAiCa nmAnAI' is – 'in my house'.

1 Gatha – Yasna – 19 – para – (2).
2 Gatha – Yasna – 52 – para – (2).

Zoroaster says – 'This house of mine, since beginning, has been abode of many Daevas and men.' Both in Avestan as well as in Vedic mythology, ancestors are revered and considered as divinities. How could Daeva be construed as something like devil or demon? 'Pitri-daeva' of Sanskrit explains the conviction that all ancestors, in Vedic world, were considered to be Daevas (lesser divinities or demi-Gods). This Avestan hymn is also attributed to all those ancestors who had lived in his house previously. They were all fore-fathers. They were all – 'Pitras'. They were all Daevas. In both worlds, they were similarly revered.

This leads us to yet another misconception. It is generally proclaimed that Zoroaster propounded a monotheistic religion that was opposed to the earlier existing polytheistic or multi-Daeva religious beliefs. We can now, in the light of facts discussed earlier, say that this presumption has no grounds. Since Avestan mythology grants space for worship of so many Daevas, it can never be considered as monotheistic. The pair 'Ahura-Mithra' is often invoked and worshipped together throughout the Zoroastrian religious texts. It shows how important both these divinities were. There are occasions in Avestan Hymns where we find the mention of – 'Mithra-Ahura'. It clearly indicates the importance of 'Mithra' in their religion and it suggests that he was not lesser, rather equally important in the Zoroastrian mythology. These two most important Zoroastrian divinities were picked up by the neighbouring civilizations as well, where they were called – 'Mica-Assira'. It appears that as the religion traveled further west, 'Mithra' got more and more importance and by the time it reached Rome, 'Ahura' was completely dropped off. Third and second century B.C. witnesses the cult of - 'Mithrium' – in Rome. In Old Persian language 'Mithra' became – 'Meher Yazd'. In fact – 'mehr-Ab' – a Persian word with religious connotations - is also related to Meher Yazd. 'Aban' is Zoroastrian concept of water. In Old Persian texts Ardvi Sur Nahid is considered to be unblemished water. She was also considered to be the consort of deity 'Mithra'. Thus, interestingly, 'Mehr-Ab' exactly means 'Mithra and Water'. The predominance of 'Mithra-Ahura' prevailed in this region for almost five thousand years. How could such a philosophy be considered – monotheistic? Zoroastrianism was, from the very beginning, a polytheistic religion.

There is yet another misconception. It is often suggested that, since all actions were possible because of knowledge or wisdom, Zoroaster named god as 'Ahur Mazda', which literally means 'The Lord Wisdom'. 'Ahura' is 'Lord' and 'Mazda' is 'Wisdom'. But reality is entirely different. Strictly according to Gatha, Lord Ahura can be identified with the Sun God. The all-important Ahura – the Sun God – clearly indicates the archaic character of this faith. The Sun was the most obvious choice of first worship in all religions of this world. It was because darkness used to be so frightening to mankind. Survival in darkness must have been a strenuous task. For men of ancient days – survival through each night would have been a traumatic experience. Rising of Sun would have been source of immense pleasure. Besides, the Sun was also the first natural and most powerful source of energy for mankind. Thus, the Sun must have been the natural first option of mankind – to be considered as the most important divinity. We find 'Ra' in Egyptian religion, 'Marduk' in Mesopotamian ancient culture and 'Ahura' in Mazdayasni religion. In almost all ancient civilizations – the Sun has been the first all-important divinity. Even Vedic religion establishes the supremacy of this most important divinity.

Ekaiva wa mahanatma dewata. Sa Surya ityachakshate.
Sa hi sarvabhutatma.

It can be translated as – 'There is only one all-important divinity. He is the Sun God. All animate and inanimate is his manifestation'. Initially, Ahur Mazda was not the name of Zoroastrian God. The Hymn of Yasna – 31 almost confirms it.

MazdI dadAT ahurO[1]

Here, 'mazdi'(mazda) is the corresponding identical of Sanskrit word – 'medha'which stands for – brightness, brilliance. In bothAvesta and Sanskrit, 'dadAT' is – gave. Thus, the aforesaid Hymn can be translated as –

This brightness (or bright rays) is given by Lord Ahura.

Therefore, we may conclude that, strictly according to Gatha, Lord Ahura was the supreme God. 'Mazda' i.e. bright rays of the day light emerged from him. The abode of Ahura – this Sun God - is always associated with eastern horizon. We have seen earlier that Ushidarvnam or the resting place of Usha – the Goddess of Dawn – was considered to be the abode of Ahura too.

It is interesting to observe some other Avestan Hymns that reveal additional information on this subject. There is a line in Yasna - 34 –

xCmAkA xCatrA ahurA fvraCVm[2]

Here 'xCmAkA' is the Sanskrit word 'KshmAkA' which means mountains. 'xCatrA' is the Sanskrit word 'KshatrA' which is region and 'fraCVm' is 'pravasam' that stands for abode or living place. Thus, it can be translated as – 'the region of mountains is the abode of Ahura'. Zoroastrians must have

1 Gatha – Yasna – 31 – para – (21).
2 Gatha – Yasna – 34 – (15).

observed the Sun emerging from behind the high peaks that was believed to be his dwelling place.

There prevails another misconception. It is about the meaning of – 'Vendidad'. Even the Avestan word 'Vendidad' is misunderstood all over. Vendidad is the religious book of Zoroastrians that came into existence in approximately fourth or fifth century BC. It is generally believed that Vendidad is the abbreviated form of 'Vi – Daevo – data'. In Zoroastrian religious texts, 'Vi-Daevo' is explained as – against Daeva (Demon) and 'data' stands for – to give. Thus, Vendidad is literally explained as the book that was given against the pre existing Daeva cult, which was the cult of Demon worship. But we have observed that Avestan 'Daeva' carried no different meaning. It was the corresponding identical of Sanskrit word – Daeva or the Latin word – Diva. Avestan 'Daeva' also meant the same. It referred to Gods. Therefore Vendidad could not be the abbreviated form of 'Vi – Daevo – data' or 'given against Gods'. It was a holy text of Zoroastrians. How could it be given against Gods?

We know that 'Va Na Tha' was a clause in Indus Valley script where 'Va' was supposed to mean dwelling place; 'Na' was light or fire and 'Tha' stood for – circle. This 'Va Na Tha' got fossilized as – 'Vana'd – in Rig Veda which meant – domestic fire. We know that worship of domestic fire is one of the most important aspects of Zoroastrian religion. Vendidad is the corresponding identical of Sanskrit word – Vana'd – i.e. domestic fire.

Zoroaster was an Indian and so was his religion. Vedic Dharma and Zoroastrian religious philosophy both developed on Indian soil. Linguistic and mythological traditions are same in both religions. None was a faith that came from outside. The seeds that developed into the earliest religions of this world were undoubtedly Indian. In its nascent stage this faith had no name. It was not Zoroastrianism because Zoroaster was not born yet. It could not be called Vedic religion because our Vedas were not yet existent. They were compiled in their present form much later. It was just a distinct faith of the inhabitants of this soil. It was magma, with no shape. It was a religion in its embryonic stage, with no name. This mother religion was, most probably, given its first name by Zoroaster himself. He named it 'Baodim' or 'Baodh'. But his followers preferred naming it Zoroastrianism, though he did not found it. He never founded any new faith. He believed in every aspect of religious philosophy, which was prevalent those days and which, later on, matured into Vedic religion. This religion in its embryonic stage had the rudiments of Vedas in it, though it took some time before Vedas could get their proper shape. It was then given the name – Vedic religion. But initially, it was all three in one. Different people named this religion of Indo-Aryans differently. It is not proper to say that Buddhism developed against Vedic religion. Buddha did not propagate any new faith that was called Baodh or Buddhism. Vedic religion itself was called Baodh any time in the fifth millennium B.C. Similarly, Zoroastrianism and early Vedic religion had no difference at all. Zoroaster lived harmoniously with Indo-Aryans. He sincerely added on to the religious beliefs of common men of his period. Observe the following line of Yasna 54 –

staot yesnya Yazamide YA dAtA aMhVuS pouruyehyA[1]

Its word by word meaning can be given as follows -

staot	-	praise
yesnya	-	Yagya
yazamide	-	worship hereby
ya	-	which

1 Gatah – Yasna – 54 – para – (2).

data	-	gave, was given
amhvus	-	to me
pouruyehya	-	predecessors

The Hymn can be translated as - 'I praise and worship hereby the holy Yagya, which was given to me by predecessors'. The corresponding identical of Avestan 'yesnya' (Yasna) is 'Yagya' in Vedic Sanskrit. Yagya used to be the religious ceremony for propitiation of divinities. It involved recitation of religious hymns and worship of fire. Haoma (Soma) and other worldly things were put into the holy flames of fire-hearths of Yagya with the belief that flames were the most suitable vehicle for transporting worldly things to Gods. These fire-hearths of Yagya ceremony were to be identified, later on, as the distinguishing characteristic feature of Aryans.

BUDDHA

Buddham sharanam gachchami

It says – I take recluse in Buddha. We are told that Siddharth got enlightened and became Buddha. And the Banyan tree under which he attained enlightenment was called 'Bodhi-tree'. But 'Bodhi' was not the common name of the species to which the tree belonged. It was 'Pipal' even before. And it still remains the same in India. Why a particular Banyan tree was named so? Was it because, under it, Buddha attained enlightenment? But why was Buddha called so? His name was Siddharth. Was it because he got enlightened under the Bodhi-tree? Who was named after whom?

It is believed that, when Gautama attained wisdom, common men named him Buddha. However, it could not, in any circumstances, become the proper name of an individual. Neither could Buddhism stand for a distinct faith. 'People were happy during the reign of the king' is an ambiguous message. Without any context, on its own, the statement does not clearify when, where or which king is referred to. Similarly, in the days of the Blessed One, even Buddha was a social term – like king. It is corroborated by the earliest Buddhist texts. Once 'Ambattha' asked his teacher as to what were the means by which he could adjudge the greatness of Gautama. His teacher – Pokkharsadi – instructed him to look for the thirty two auspicious body signs of great men, about which scriptures declared – ' if a man has those and if he dwells at home he will become a sovereign in this world; but if he goes away from the household life into the houseless state, then he will become a Buddha.' It shows that Buddha was the highest stage that could be attained by an individual in the world of religion, just as the sovereign was in this material world. It was in this sense that common men, who followed Vedic scriptures, used the word –Buddha - during the days of the Blessed One. Even in the religious texts of Jainism, which certainly preceded Gautama, the word Buddha was generally used in the sense of an 'acharya' or 'teacher'. Thus, in the days of the Blessed One, 'Buddha' was a general term attributed to any religious teacher of repute by followers of Jainism. Strictly according to religious texts of Jainism, even Lord Mahavir was a Buddha. Even his philosophy could be called Buddhism. Thus, the term – Buddha - could only be used indiscriminately for religious teachers – without ever clarifying the creed to which the teacher belonged. Therefore, 'I take recluse in Buddhism' could not be related to a particular faith. It could have certainly lead to confusion. In fact Gautama himself could not have sanctioned its use. He was a genius. He even permitted the use of local languages to facilitate easy comprehension and dissemination of the tenets of Dhamma. To use Buddhism – in this sense – could breed confusion. It would have been more appropriate to name his religion as – 'Siddharthism' or 'Gautamism'. There appears no rationale to describe the religion of Gautama distinctly as Buddhism. Or was it something else?

'Buddham' – as discussed earlier, was the general word for any religious teacher of repute, in Jaina religion. It could also be a Vedic saint with thirty-two auspicious body signs. Therefore 'I take recluse in Buddha' could not, on its own, specify the distinct faith of the follower. Neither could 'Buddham' be associated only with Gautama. And yet, somehow, people had no confusion. To them, 'Buddham' conveyed a specific meaning. It was related to a distinct faith.

Similarly, 'sangham' stands for congregation, viharas, mathas or union of a group of people. 'Nairyo sangham' of

Avestan texts conveys the union or body that was constituted by females of the society. We even had 'Jaina sangha' that was the place of residence of the followers of Jainism. Sangham on its own does not convey any particular faith. But observe the following line -

Sangham sharanam gachchhami

It says – I take recluse in Sangha. This 'sangha' could be of any type. It could be the body of females – Nairyo Sangham. It could also mean – a Jaina Monastary. But Gautama used this word for 'mathas' or 'viharas' of a particular faith signifying only Buddhist monks and the governing instruments thereof. It could not be mistaken to be any other type of union. Message was clear – inspite of the fact that the identity of the type of Sangha is nowhere disclosed. It proves that this 'Sangham' was not something new in the society. Common people were familiar with its specific meaning. It was just the Buddhist Sangha – and nothing else. To them, it exactly meant- 'I undertake to live with and abide by the rules of Buddhist monastery'.

Even 'Dhamma' was the general word for religion. It is the corresponding identical of Sanskrit – 'Dharma', which stands for religion. Thus, 'Dhammam' in the following line does not imply any particular creed -

Dhammam sharanam Gachchhami

It can be translated exactly as-'I take recluse in religion'. Here the message ought to be ambiguous. Even during the days of the Blessed One, India was not bereft of multiple religious doctrines. Besides Vedic religion and Jainism, there were many other philosophers in society, who pursued different doctrines. Therefore, 'I take recluse in religion' becomes a general statement. It is not specific. The name or the identity of the creed has to be there to make the statement meaningful. Yet, somehow, people had no confusion. To them, this Dhamma was only Buddhism. For them – Dhamma was a distinct faith.

Although 'Buddham', 'Dhammam' and 'Sangham' – could have been used indiscriminately in society during the days of Gautama, yet, on the contrary, it was absolutely clear to common people that all three terms were related to just a single distinct faith. Why? What reason did they have to presume so? Why did it not lead to confusion – even during and after the days of Gautama? It was so because, most probably, things were absolutely clear in society. Gautama was talking to common men – in their own language. He used words that were clearly understood by them and about which they had no confusion. It was possible only when the three terms, with their specific meanings, pre-existed Gautama. Only then could he use it so easily. Only then was he not required to reveal the context before using – 'Buddham', 'Dhammam' or 'Sangham'.

Dhamma had no relation with the Blessed One. We know that Avesta speaking Zoroastrians were Indians and a significant part of their sacred hymns were compiled here on Indian soil. We know that even Zoroaster was born here. Observe the following lines of Avestan texts -

Dhammam narvam aCaonam aise Yesti

It says - 'Dhamma is the shelter of mankind. So it is.' These lines preceded Buddha by at least three thousand years. In those days, Dhamma was not the general term for any religion. It meant a distinct faith. It did not require any name because, in those early days, there did not exist any other religious philosophy. Dhamma was the magma that, later on, evolved to become the earliest religion of the world. Zoroaster gave it a name -'Baodim' or 'Baodh'. He even defined 'Baodh-karma'. We have seen earlier that all thoughts, speech and actions benevolent to humanity were declared 'Baodh-Karma'

(Buddhist acts) by Zoroaster. Similarly, all thoughts, speech and deeds that were malevolent to the world were declared against 'Baodh-Karma' (non Buddhist acts). People were quite familiar with this 'Baodh' religion since time immemorial. Strictly according to Avestan texts, 'Baodh' or 'Baodi' was the name of the religion that was given by Ahura.Therefore, we may conclude that the so called 'Baodh Dhamma' pre-existed Gotama. It was prevalent since atleast three thousand years before our Buddha (Gotama) was born. Observe the following line of Khordeh Avesta –

Ahum cha daenam cha baodhas cha[1]

'Ahum cha' is – my or mine. 'Daenam cha' stands for – religion. 'Baodhas cha' can be translated as – Baodh. The hymn says –

Baodh is the name of my religion.

But now we come to a very important aspect of our history. Kushinagar and Gaya are the two places, which are significantly related with the life of Zoroaster. But these are, surprisingly, the most important places related with Buddha's life too. According to Avestan texts, in all probability, Zoroaster got enlightened at Kushinagar and died at Gaya. On the other hand, Buddha got enlightened at Gaya and breathed his last at Kushinagar. This is strange. I refuse to consider it a mere coincidence. Greatness is a rare commodity and its recurrence at any particular place is absurd. We ought to reason things out. Since Buddha came almost three thousand years after Zoroaster, to dig into the circumstances that led Buddha to Gaya and Kushinagar shall be the logical course of action. The foremost important question is – why did Buddha choose to go to Gaya in his pursuit of knowledge? Was Gaya, in those days, an important seat of learning? No Vedic or Buddhist

1 Khordeh Avesta – Kardo in memory of departed.

texts have ever indicated that Gaya was one such place. Rather, since time immemorial, Kashi (Varanasi) had been the most important seat of learning where scholars used to gather, to take part in various religious discourses. But, initially, Buddha never went there. We are told that, in his pursuit of knowledge, he kept wandering from place to place. He had gone to the abode of Arad Kamal who taught the doctrine of self renunciation. Arad Kamal had a great number of followers and all of them lead lives of great austerity. But Siddhartha saw the vanity of the doctrine and decided to leave his hermitage. Then he had gone to Rajgriha – a famous place near Pataliputra – where lived Udrak Ram Putra. Udrak Ram Putra was a philosopher of repute those days. But the explanations offered by him did not convince Siddhartha. Finally, Siddhartha, along with five other disciples of Udrak Ram Putra decided to proceed to Gaya. Even these five disciples – Kaundinya, Ashvajit, Vashpa, Mahanaman and Bhadrika had become disenchanted by the doctrine of Udrak Ram Putra. All six of them had become friends and they together decided to go to Gaya in pursuit of truth. Why? What was there in Gaya? One thing is absolutely clear – they were certainly not aimless wanderers. They must have had definite reasons to proceed to Gaya.

We are told that Buddha and these five sages together took to intense meditation at Gaya. Why? Siddhartha had no reason to do that. He had left the hermitage of Arad Kamal with certain conviction. He had realized there that severe austerity and philosophy of self-renunciation was futile. It was painful and hence, it could not be the means of true salvation. Therefore he had decided to search for the path himself that could lead to the state of ultimate bliss. And yet, after reaching the banks of river Nairanjana in Gaya, he started practicing sever austerity which lead to painful self – mortification. He kept on reducing his daily meal till he started living off a single grain. This weakened his body so badly that he could barely manage his way in the streams of the river. Now, this is strange. How could he start practicing the same doctrine of painful mortification, which he had himself rejected earlier? Nay, that seems unbelievable.

Buddhist scriptures describe that finally Siddhartha gave up this painful and severe austerity. He started eating well – to gain strength. But his friends did not think it wise. They finally gave up and proceeded to Sarnath (a place in Kashi), where they thought enlightenment could be achieved. There we are! Since ages, Kashi had been a famous seat of learning. They thought the key to salvation might be there in Vedic philosophy. Hence they came to Kashi. But Siddharth never went to Kashi in pursuit of truth. Why? And what led him initially to Gaya? What reason did his friends have to proceed to Gaya – after they got disenchanted with the philosophy of Udrak Ram Putra? Was it the center stage of some other sect? Could it be that, besides Vedic religion, there existed yet another philosophy, of which Gaya was the most important center? Because one thing is absolutely clear – they never wandered aimlessly. They kept moving to all those places where they thought they could attain the ultimate wisdom. What was there in Gaya, in those ancient days, which attracted them?

We know that Zoroaster was the first Prophet of mankind. He had died at Gaya. Therefore, Gaya must have become one of the earliest centres of pilgrimage for the followers of Avestan religion. Here, must have thrived the earliest philosophy of this world – Baodim. Could it be that 'Bodhi tree' was not any tree at all? Probably, it was the 'Bodhi – Shakha' of Indian philosophy. 'Shakha' means 'branch' and Gaya was the place where 'Bodhi – Sect' or 'Bodhi – branch' had been flourishing since Zoroaster's days. Siddhartha studied this Bodhi branch of philosophy, got enlightened under it and was, therefore, named as Buddha.

'Uruvella' was the exact place where Gotama got enlightened. Let us observe things as they were when the Blessed one had reached Uruvella. Uruvella was the land of Jatilas. The chief of Jatilas was 'Kassap'. Their faith was treated with regards in Magadha. Even Bimbisara was the follower of Jatilas. According to Buddhist accounts, later on, Kassapa had become follower of the Blessed One. The declaration of Kassap is preserved in Buddhist texts. He said - 'the profit I derived from adoring the Fire was continuance of the wheel of individuality, with all its sorrows and vanities. This service I have cast away.' Thus, formerly, Kassapa was a 'Fire' worshipper. It indicates that Uruvela – where river Nairanjana flows; where Siddhartha got enlightened – was inhabited by people who worshipped Fire. They were indeed the followers of Ahura's religion – Baodim. The worship of eternal flame was practiced at Uruvella and it was here that the Blessed One got enlightened. How interesting? Almost similar incident had taken place roughly thousand years before Siddhartha was born. 'Torah' is the words of God revealed to Moses. It is the most important document of Judaism and the word 'Torah' in 'Hebrew' language is explained as – teachings, instructions or laws. According to 'Genesis', Moses reached Media in exile, where he lived as a shepherd. He used to feed his sheep on Mount Horeb. It was on top of this mountain in Media that, on a particular day, God appeared to him through 'a burning bush' that failed to extinguish. It was the 'Eternal Flame'. We know that, by early second millennium B.C., Zoroastrianism was established in the regions of Media. Divine revelation was made to Moses through this Eternal Flame. The story doesn't end here. Moses was bestowed with the famous – stone tablets. And along with it, he was given intricate and elaborate instructions regarding maintenance of – 'Menorah' – the eternal flame, which was supposed to be preserved in each temple in such manner that it would never get extinguished and that it would have incessant supply of oil – for burning.

It is, indeed, interesting to observe the similarities of the most ancient religions of this world. Moses is considered as a Prophet in all three religions - Judaism, Christianity and Islam. The relation does not stop here. It extends further. Another resemblance lies in the mystical number – 72. Zoroastrian Gatha has seventy-two chapters. Zoroastrians consider this number as most auspicious. Each Zoroastrian is supposed to wear 'Kushti' or the 'Sacred Girdle' around waist. It is made up of seventy-two threads of lamb's wool, which represent seventy-two chapters of holy religious text. Thus, each Zoroastrian virtually carries on his body – the symbolic seventy-two threads of Kushti, which represents complete Gathic text itself. In Kabbalah – which was the religious faith of people of Middle East in thirteenth century B.C., and which is no different from early Judaism – there are exactly seventy-two names of the God Almighty. Even in Mohamdan religion there are seventy-two different sects.

But let us come back to the religion of Uruvela. Ahura's religion – Baodim - was almost three to four thousand years old. Isn't that stretch of period too long? Long enough – for the philosophy to be rendered archaic? Even the language needed a facelift. The religious doctrine had become incomprehensible to general mass. The basics of this archaic religion had to be mouthed a new so that people could cast their doubts. No wonder that we find in this Anga – Magadha terrain, so many philosophers in that era. Purana Kassap, Makkhali ghoshal, Ajit Keshkambal, Udrak Ram putra and Mahavira were a few of them – all experimenting something new. The Blessed One was also one of them.

Let us now get into the circumstances that brought Kushinara or kushinagar into significance. It is mentioned in Maha Parinibban Sutta of Diggha Nikaya that Buddha, during his stay at Vaisali, had declared that he was going to die three months hence. This decision was clearly conveyed to Mara – the evil one – who had come to take him away. Thus, Buddha chose a certain time for his Parinibban. Similarly, for this Parinibban, he chose a specific place too. It was Kushinagar. But what was so special about this place? Ananda was one of the closest disciples of Buddha. He was present with the Blessed One during the last days. Even he was puzzled. There were many significant places like Rajgrih, Vaisali, Pataliputra, Gaya or Sravasti, and any one of these could have been a better place for the Maha Parinibban of the Blessed One. Ananda even inquired about it. But Buddha told him that long - long ago, there at Kushinara, lived a noble king - 'Maha Sudassan' – whose name and fame was far reached. Thus, it was in no way an insignificant place. Isn't that strange?

Even if it was the abode of the famous noble king Maha Sudassan, does it, in any way, justify the merit of this particular place for Buddha's Maha Parinibban? Ajatshatru - the famous Magadha king - was the greatest king of his time. He was contemporary to, as well as, a follower of Buddha. His capital Rajgrih could have been a better choice. Even Ananda had pointed it out. Buddha's birthplace Sravasti was very close to Kushinara. It was just a hundred kilometers away. Even that could have been a better option. The justification put forth for selection of this particular place – Kushinara – is not convincing. The Vajjies of Vaisali were his most favoured followers. They sincerely deserved to witness this greatest incident of their time – Maha Parinibban of their God. But for Buddha, it seems, nothing could be compared with the importance of Kushinara. No worldly merit of Rajgrih, Vaisali,

Sravasti or Gaya could considerably withstand as much, to change Buddha's decision. Why? Not simply because it had been the place of residence of some famous king who had ruled some hundreds of years before Buddha's period. It was not the sufficient cause. The place of Maha Parinibban had to be a very sacred place. There had to be the commissioning of some act, religious or mythological, which could render Kushinara sacred. And there, indeed, it was. Kushinagar had been the place of enlightenment of Zoroaster. The incident took place almost three thousand years before Buddha. It must have been a famous place of pilgrimage of Zoroastrians. It could be a place of pilgrimage for Buddha too, for even he was a student of Baodim. No wonder Buddha preferred to breathe his last at this holy place.

According to Buddhist traditions 'Pali' is regarded as the language that Shakhyamuni spoke. Hence, they called it – 'the fundamental' language. But there seems to remain a persistent confusion about inter- relation between Pali and the language that was spoken in the ancient kingdom of Magadha. Besides, the significant similarity of Pali with the language Avesta has also been bewildering. Some scholars considered it as a mid-Indo-European language. But it was rightly observed that Pali was not a direct descendent of Vedic Sanskrit. And here originated the main confusion. Till date, scholars have not been able to classify this language. They have had only two choices. They could put it either in Indo-European family or in Indo-Aryan family of languages. But it could not be regarded as an Indo-Aryan language because it was not a direct descendent of Vedic Sanskrit. Nor could they trace it to Indo-European stalk because of the geographical belts where this language was prevalent. It was embedded deep inside the peninsular India and reached as far as Sri Lanka and Burma. And at the same time, it was not the vernacular of Northern Indian plains.

But the main question is – when did such migration of speakers of this new language of Indo-European family take place? How could it bypass North India? How could the same language be prevalent in two different parts of world – Iran and peninsular regions of India - that were separated by a long stretch of Sanskrit speaking Aryans? They had no way to explain. Therefore, we are left with no other choice but to consider the opposite to be true. We know that Avesta, Sanskrit and Pali evolved from a common root. It all originated from the language of Bavra people. It clearifies why Pali betrays the fact that it has descended from Sanskrit and yet, it carries enough linguistic similarities to Vedic Sanskrit. It was not because Sanskrit words were incorporated in due course. It was because Sanskrit and Pali had evolved from the same stalk.

But Pali was not the mother tongue of Buddha. Yet, after his enlightenment, he preached in Pali. Why? Was his religion meant only for Pali speaking population of Magadha? We are told that Buddhism was a reaction against Hindu perversions. It was a reform that challenged the efficacy of Brahmanic rites and ceremonies that had taken roots in the society. But if it was so, then Buddha had all the more reasons to come back to the Vedic world and preach them in their own language. Pali could not be understood easily in Vedic world or Hindu society. How could Buddha prove the supremacy of his philosophy? How could he use Pali to satisfy the curiosity of newcomers? How could he use Pali to prove the underlying felicity of Vedic beliefs of that time? However, one thing is absolutely clear. His newfound philosophy was not meant only for Magadha. Otherwise, he would not have traveled all the way to Varanasi (Sarnath) to give his first sermon. In those days, Varanasi was the philosophical center of Vedic religion. But what made him learn Pali in the first place? He could not have done it without purpose. It is obvious that he did not intend to keep his newfound faith restricted to Pali speaking area. Therefore, the only reason that can be attributed to this act is – compulsion. To learn Pali must have been a necessary factor for attainment of enlightenment. It is obvious then that Buddha had gone into the non-Sanskritic Pali world to understand their culture and religion. Magadha was the religious and philosophical school of Buddha. It was different. To understand it, he had to have mastery over their language. Therefore, he learnt Pali. He studied their religion and perhaps, got answers to all his queries. He was enlightened. But his philosophical thought world was filled with this new language. He had inherited the thought process of a different culture in a different language. He was born a new. Here after he could not avoid using Pali words to express the subtle design of newfound doctrine. The use of Pali words, laden with cultural and religious overtones was necessary to convey exact meaning. Enlightened Buddha had no option but to profess his religion in Pali. Religion of Bavra world was the religion of Magadha. It was more than three thousand years old. He had studied this religion of Bavra world. He had read the contents of Zoroastrian Gatha. He was enlightened in this ancient religion – 'Baodim'. And he mouthed it anew.

There is an interesting history of the so-called 'middle-path' of Buddhism. The Blessed One has been credited with this philosophy of 'middle- path'. It is commonly believed to be the balanced state between two available extremes. On one hand it forbids people from seeking salvation through sever austerity and on the other, it condemns indulgence in worldly pleasures. These are the two extremes and the ideal state of existence would be somewhere in between. Buddha preached that satisfying the necessities of life was not evil. The restrained existence – which barely sustains the basic needs of life, and which lacks greed or lust for rest of worldly things, is the ideal state for a hermit. This is the Middle Path – devoid of both extremes. It condemns both - lust for material world and painful self mortification. The Blessed One called it – 'Majjhima Patipada'. The corresponding identical word of Majjhima is 'Madhyama' in Sanskrit. It stands for – middle. Similarly, the Sanskrit equivalent of 'Patipada' is – Pratipada. Pratipada means – path. Together – Madhyama Pratipada – stands for Middle Path. 'Majjhima Patipada' and 'Madhyama Pratipada' is one and the same. Surprisingly, we get similar expression in Zoroastrian scriptures as well. In Avestan texts, we often come across – 'Maidhyo- Paitishtanas cha'. The corresponding Sanskrit equivalent of Avestan 'Maidhyo' is – Madhyo – that is 'middle'. Similarly, 'Paitishtan' is nothing but Sanskrit 'Pratishthan'. We know that Sanskrit 'prati' always becomes 'paiti' in Avesta. The Sanskrit word 'Pratishthanam' stands for – state of being. Thus, 'Maidhyo-Paitishtanas cha' of Sarosh Yasht of Khordeh Avesta can be translated as – being in a state which is in the middle, which is equi-distant. Is there any difference between the 'Majjhima Patipada' of Pali texts and 'Maidhyo-Paitishtanas cha' of Avestan texts? There is no space for any doubts. The philosophy of 'Middle Path' was given by Zoroaster. Buddha came almost three thousand years after Zoroaster. In Yasna – 22 we observe the following line –

aEsm&s ca baoiDIm ca Ayese Yesti[1]

The meaning of 'aEsm&s' is interesting. Here, the word qualifies – 'baoiDim', which is the name of the religion given by Lord Ahura. In 'aEsm&s', the root word is 'sm' or 'sam'. This word is identically present in Sanskrit as well. In Sanskrit the word 'sam' also means – situated at equi-distance or situated in the middle.This was the famous 'Middle Path' of Avesta.

1 Gatha – Yasna – 22 – para – (3).

Zoroastrian 'Baodim' was 'Aesam'. 'Ayese Yesti' is translated as – so it is. 'Baodim' was the philosophy of – 'Middle Path'.

Similarly, The Eight Fold Path of Buddha is the way of life designed to overcome the miseries of existence. It is described as follows -

Samma Dithi (View)
Samma Sankappo (Resolve)
Samma Vaacha (Speech)
Samma Kammanto (Action)
Samma Ajivo (Livelihoods)
Samma Vayamo (Effort)
Samma Sati (Mindfulness)
Samma Samadhi (Concentration)

The living guided by these eight pillars, according to the Blessed One, is the way to ultimate state of bliss – called 'Nirvana'. But strangely enough, even Avestan texts have something that is exactly similar to this Eight Fold Path, although, till date, it has been explained somewhat differently. We come across an Avestan expression – 'astvaitim gaetham'. It is there in 'Sraosh Yasht' of 'Khordeh Avesta. It exists frequently throughout Zoroastrian religious texts. In Persian books, the word – astvaitim or astvaitam – is explained as the corresponding identical of 'asthivat' of Sanskrit language. 'Asthi' in Sanskrit is – skeleton or bones. 'Astvaitim' is believed to stand for 'corporeal' or 'made of bones'. Similarly, 'gaetham' is explained to have originated from the root word – 'gi'- which is 'to live'. Its relative meaning is given as – world. Thus, together, the two words – 'astvaitim gaetham' – have been translated as 'the material world' or 'the corporeal existence'. But this can not be the true meaning of either 'astvaitim' or 'gaetham'. The hymns of Gatha make it amply clear that 'gaethyai' or 'gaetham' could not be 'the corporeal existence' or 'the material world'. In Yasna – 16 we come across the Avestan expression – 'Yazat gaEqyAica'. Here the word 'gaEqyAica' is pronounced as 'gaEthyAi cha'. We know that 'Yazat' is the verb that denotes the act of worship or reverence. Its root word is 'Yaz', which is identically found in Sanskrit as well. In Avesta, the lesser divinities are also called – 'Yazats'. 'cha' is a word common in both Avesta and Sanskrit. It generally stands for – 'too'. Therefore, 'Yazat gaEqyAica' can be translated as – 'We worship gaEthyAi too'. How can 'gaEthyAi' be anything like 'material world' or 'corporeal existence'? 'We worship the material world' or 'we worship the corporeal existence' goes against every norm of Zoroastrian philosophy. It just can not be true. Therefore, 'gaEthyAi' or 'gaetham' is not a word that could mean – corporeal, world etc. 'Gaetham' or 'gaEthyAi' relates to something that is worthy of reverence. 'Gaetham' is 'Gatha' itself. The true meaning of 'Yazat gaEthyAi cha' is –

We worship Gatha too.

Similarly, we have many instances in Avestan hymns, where this word 'gaetham' is paired with 'fraadat'. Zoroastrian religious books explain this 'fraadat gaetham' as 'bringing prosperity to the world'. According to them, 'Fraadat' is 'prosperity' and 'gaetham' is 'world'. But 'fraadat' is the corresponding identical of Sanskrit word 'pradat' that is – 'to give'. And it is interesting to note that, at almost all other places in Gatha, Avestan word 'fraadat' is used to exactly convey the same sense i.e. 'to give'. Therefore, 'fraadat gaetham' can not be – 'bringing prosperity to the world'. Its true meaning would be – 'gave Gatha (to us)'. In 'Ushahen Geh' of 'Khordeh Avesta' we come across –

Verethrajane fradat gaethahe[1]

1 Khordeh Avesta – Ushahen Geh – para – (2).

The word 'verethraghna' of Gatha is often written as 'verethrajane' in later Avestan texts. Here, in this hymn too, 'verethrajane' is the erroneous transcription of – 'verethraghna'. We know that Avestan word 'verethraghna' stands for – 'killing of darkness'. In Zoroastrian scriptures we find 'verethraghna' often used as the epithet of the most important Zoroastrian divinity i.e. Sun God. We have its corresponding identical word in Vedic mythology as well. The corresponding identical of Avestan 'verethraghna' is – 'vritraghna'. 'Verethrajane fradat gaethahe' exactly means –

For removal of ignorance Gatha was bestowed to us.

Or

For removal of darkness you gave us Gatha

Now observe the following hymn of Yasna – 57 of Avestan Gatha which clearly indicates the meaning of 'astwaitim gaetham'.

WasO xCaqrO fracarAiti[1]
aoi Y&m astwaitIm gaEq&m
aya daEnaya fraorvaNta
ahurO mazdI aCawa

The word – by – word meaning of this hymn is as follows–

WasO	–	to live, living
xCathro	–	land, area, empire
fracarAiti	–	propagate, spread
aOi Yam	–	this is
astwaitIm gaEtham	–	?
aya	–	this
daEnaya	–	religion
fraorvaNta	–	to give, spread
ahuro mazdI aCawa	–	Lord Ahura Mazda

1 Gatha – Yasna – 57 – para – (24).

Now the whole thing stands as – 'which has been propagated all over living world – this is Astvaitim Gaetham – this is the religion given by Lord Ahura.' Here 'Astvaitim Gaetham' has to be some kind of religious philosophy. It cannot be 'the material world' or 'the corporeal existence'. It has to be a religious doctrine.

Let us now, analyse the word 'Astvaitim'. It is a compound word. It is made up of 'ast' and 'vaitim'. 'ast' is the corresponding identical of Sanskrit word – 'asht'. 'ast' or 'asht' is the number 'Eight'. In Vendidad (Fargard – IV – 14), eight hundred is written as – 'ast sata'.'vaitim' is the corresponding identical of Sanskrit word – 'vrittim'. Even here, Sanskrit 'r' gets replaced, as usual, by the Avestan 'ai'. In Sanskrit, 'vritti' stands for 'way of life' or 'path'. 'Astvaitim' exactly means – Eight Fold Path. 'Gaetham' is 'of Gatha'. Together, 'Astvaitim Gaetham' can be translated as – the Eight Fold Path of the Gatha. Here we have a true religious philosophy. Now it fits well with the context. This was the doctrine propagated by Zoroaster. This was the religion given by Lord Ahura. Isn't that a forerunner of Eight Fold Path of Lord Buddha? This hymn of Yasna – 57 can be translated as –

Propagated all over living world
This is the Eight Fold Path of Gatha
This was the religion given to us
By Lord Ahur Mazda

Now observe the following line of Khordeh Avesta (Jasa me avanghe Mazda) –

Aeshe asti Daenayao Mazdayasnoish astuitish[1]

'Aeshe asti' can be translated as – so it is. 'Daenayao' is religion and 'Mazdayasnoish astuitish' stands for – the eight

1 Khordeh Avesta – Din-No-Kalmo (Avesta) – para – (8).

fold path of Mazdayasni religion. This was the eight fold path of Gatha. This was the eight fold path of Mazdayasni religion. This line is also mentioned at many other places like – Din-No-Kalmo etc. This Eight-Fold Path of Avestan text is fully illustrated in Yasna – 12. It goes like this –

AstuyE humatvm manO[1]
AstuyE hUxtvm WacO
AstuyE hwarStvm Kyaoqanvm
AstuyE daEn&m mazdAyasnIm
fraspAyaoxvDr&m
niDAsnaiqiCvm
XaEtwadaq&m
aCaonIm

Zoroastrians worshipped Ahura. That is why people called it Ahuiric religion. They worshipped Mazda – the bright rays of the Sun. Hence, the religion was also called Mazdayasni religion. But the actual name of their religion was – 'Baodh'. It was the religion of Zoroaster. It was the religion of the ancient Bavra world. Baodh was the first religious philosophy of Indian soil. Aryans and Hinduism came much later.

---

1 Gatha – Yasna – 12 – para – (8&9).

Caste System of Indo-Iranians

The existence of a functional hierarchical system of division of mankind is the characteristic feature of Indian societies since time immemorial. 'Varna' and 'Jati' are the two terms distinctly used in later Vedic texts to describe this system of social stratification. 'Varna-vyawastha' is the system of classification on the basis of 'Varna'. Similarly, 'Jati-vyawastha' is the system of classification on the basis of different 'Jati'. Till date, much confusion has been made about the meaning of 'Varn' and 'Jati'. We are told that these were two different things. 'Jati' or caste was a social differentiation where as 'Varna' or class was the economic stratification of the members of the society. 'Jati' was an endogamous social group. 'Varna' was a group of people occupying, more or less, similar social status. One was of permanent nature where as the other was fluid in nature. 'Varna' was the broad general economic and occupational classification that distinguished the members of society into four distinct groups – 'Brahmans', 'Kshatriyas', 'Vaishyas' and 'Shudras'. But 'Jati' was a diversified system of social classification of individuals. It involved further sub-division of the four 'Varnas' into distinct identifiable sub-groups. They were plenty in number.

Thus, before we proceed any further, it is important to understand what exactly, could have been the meaning of 'Varna' and 'Jati' in context of ancient Indian civilization. We get the earliest mention of the four-fold 'Varna-vyawastha' in the famous 'Purush-Sukta' of tenth 'Mandala' of Rig-Veda. It lays down the theory of divine origin of the four 'Varnas'. It says that 'Brahmans', Kshatriyas', 'Vaishyas' and 'Shudras' sprang respectively from the mouth, arms, thighs and feet of the

Divine Being. This is the first instance where we get the names of all four 'Varnas' of ancient Vedic world. But 'Purush-Sukta' of Rig-Veda does not use the word 'Varna' itself. Therefore, we do not know what these four-fold divisions of mankind were called in early Vedic days. In fact the word 'Varna' is used in Rig-Veda quite a number of times. But nowhere does it refer to the four-fold system of stratification. 'Varna' in Rig-Vedic Hymns generally means 'colour' or 'light'. Observe the following Hymn of Rig-Veda -

Yo Dasam Varnamadharam Guha Kah[1]

It says – Lord Indra caused the colour of Dasas to be retained inside a dark cave. Here, 'Varna' has been used to signify the colour of skin of Dasas. 'Varna', in Rig-Vedic Hymns does not signify the four-fold social stratification. It is in Atharva-Veda where we get the first mention of 'Varna' in the sense of a system of four-fold hierarchical division. From here on, we get the true mention of four-fold 'Varna-vyawastha' that divides the members of society into four compartments called – 'Varnas'. But Rig-Vedic Hymns present a different picture of the society. Apart from 'Purush-Sukta' we do not get the mention of all four 'Varnas' anywhere else in Rig-Veda. Some scholars are also of the opinion that the tenth Mandala of Rig-Veda that contains 'Purush-Sukta' is not the part of original text. It is considered to be the work of some later period that was added to the original text of Rig-Veda. However, without getting into the authenticity of the tenth Mandala, we may reasonably conclude that, since no other Hymn of Rig-Veda mentions about the four 'Varnas' of the society, the four-fold Varna classification was non-existent in early Vedic period. Although terms like 'Brahman' and 'Rajanya' are used in Rig-Vedic Hymns, but even they do not convey the sense of any

1 Rig Veda – 2 – 12 – (2120).

distinct 'Varna'. It proves that Rig-Vedic society did not have the four-fold classification called – 'Varna-vyawastha'.

However, Vedic people were distinctly divided into two compartments – Aryans and Dasas. Dasas were non-Aryans. They could be distinguished from Aryans on the basis of certain features that are clearly mentioned in Rig-Vedic Hymns. Firstly, Dasas were considered to be – 'Abratas'. It revealed the first important characteristic that differentiated Dasas from Aryans. 'Abratas' stands for non-followers of rites and rituals of Vedic Gods. Secondly, Dasas were called – 'Akratus' i.e. persons who did not perform holy 'Yagya' or 'Havana'. 'Yagya' or 'Havana' was the distinct trait of Aryans. Thirdly, Dasas were called – 'Apnasah'. 'Apanasah' can be translated as persons whose shape of nose is flat in comparison to the sharp, erect and prominent nose of Aryans. Fourthly, Dasas were believed to be – 'Mridhra-Vachah'. 'Mridhra-Vachah' can be translated as persons whose speech is not clear and melodious. It is interesting to note that Aryans and Dasas are distinguished here merely on the basis of clarity and accent of speech. They are not considered to be speaking different language. Fifthly, Aryans and Dasas could also be differentiated on the basis of colour of skin. Dasas were people with dark complexion. Now this distinguishing feature does bear a direct relation to the Rig-Vedic term 'Varna' i.e. colour. We may conclude that, strictly according to Rig-Vedic Hymns, 'Varna' or colour was one of the distinguishing characteristic feature on the basis of which members of society were divided into two distinct class or caste or group. Therefore, Rig-Vedic 'Varna-vyawastha' or system of classification on the basis of colour of skin could have only two groups or classes – fair and dark. Aryans possessed fair skin colour. In contrast, Dasas were dark complexioned. Could it be that in early Vedic days society was divided into only two-fold 'Varna-vyawastha'? Could it be that, initially, 'Varna-vyawastha' did not refer to occupation or social position in terms of wealth and education? I think so. 'Varna' i.e. colour was the basis of distinction and accordingly, we had only two 'Varna' groups or classes. It was in the later days that the same term 'Varna' was used for the four distinct occupational classes or castes. It was the continuation of old practice. Since 'Varna' was the basis of classification in Rig-Vedic period, the use of the same term 'Varna' was continued for distinct occupational groups of the society of later days.

Rig-Vedic society had a distinct two-fold 'Varn-vyawastha'. This is clear from the following Hymn of Rig Veda, which says –

Ubhao Varnavrishirugrah puposhati

It describes – the sage wished for both Varnas. Here 'Varna' is not used to convey the sense of colour. The number of colours is not restricted to two. They are plenty. 'Ubhao Varna' or 'both colours' is an absurd expression unless preceded or followed by a clarification. It can be used only when any two particular colours have been clearly selected and spelt out in the context. But this Vedic Hymn does not have any such context. It does not indicate which of the two colours, from the vast spectrum of available shades, is the sage wishing about. There is no mention of any two particular colours or shades. Yet the sage is said to have wished both 'Varnas'. It is absolutely clear, therefore, that there is no confusion about the number of 'Varnas'. They are not plenty. They are just two in number and that the sage wishes for both of them. What else could it be? 'Varnas', in this passage are the two classes or castes – Aryans and non-Aryans (Dasas).

It is generally believed that 'Varna' or class was the system of economic stratification where as 'Jati' or caste dealt with the system of social differentiation. Since ages, much confusion has been made about it. Even in 'Manu-Smriti', the term 'Varna', at some places, conveys the meaning of 'Jati' where as, at other places it is used to convey the sense of a mixed group of 'Jati'. However, if we take a look into the ancient Avestan texts, we get some interesting and definite clues on this subject. According to Gatha, the primitive Avestan society was distinctly divided into two broad groups – Aryans and Bavras. Bavras were non- Aryans. It was exactly similar to the scheme of differentiation of Rig-Vedic society. The only difference was that, in Avesta, non-Aryans were called Bavras where as, in Rig-Veda, they were called Dasas. But Aryans and Bavras of the Avestan world were not considered to be two 'Varnas'. Bavra was a 'Jati'. And so was Arya. They were considered to be two distinct 'Jati'. Observe the following Avestan hymn of Gatha -

Zaoqra haDa barvsma Ayese Yesti[1]

It says – 'By Jati (caste) we are Bavra. So it is.' 'Zaoqra' (Zaotra) stands for – class or caste.

Barvsma haDa zaoqra Ayese Yesti[2]

This Avestan line can be translated as – 'Because we are Bavra, that is our Jati (caste). So it is.'

Thus, we may conclude that Rig-Vedic 'Arya-Dasa' divide was the corresponding identical of 'Arya-Bavra' classification of Avestan world. In Avestan Gatha, these Aryans and non-Aryans (Bavras) constituted two distinct 'Jati'.We know that Avesta speaking people were Indians. Therefore, we may also presume that 'Varna' and 'Jati' – both terms were in use simultaneously and that they were synonyms. In all probability, 'Jati' was used in non-Aryan or Bavra or Dasa world. We find its use in Avestan, Pali and all other important Indian languages. Sanskrit speaking Aryans used 'Varna'.

1 Gatha – Yasna – 2 – para – (1).
2 Gatha – Yasna – 2 – para – (1).

These Bavra people can be identified with the 'Bavru', 'Briwi', 'Bratya' or 'Dasa' of Vedic and later Vedic literature. Its antonym is 'Arya'. In all probability, that was the way ancient Indian society was divided. The group that preferred tribal way of living was called Bavra, whereas the lot, that preferred living in villages and towns and took to agriculture and trade, was called Arya. They were not of different races. Difference was only due to ways of living and it was not mutually exclusive. With the passage of time more and more people took to the comfort of agriculture. Gradually forests were cleared to get more agricultural land. Bavra way of living became a thing of past. Most of the Bavra population took to Aryan way of living.

Now, let us observe the other system of classification of society that had yielded four-fold occupational groups. It was often wrongly advocated that four-fold system of classification was the outcome of inter-racial cultural interaction and synthesis between invading Aryans and non-Aryans and that non-Aryans were natives of this land. We know that even Bavra world was distinctly divided into four occupational classes or castes. Aryans in no way affected this development of Bavra world. Rather, Bavra society preceded the process of Aryanization. And the essence of process of Aryanisation lay in adopting the profession of agriculture and trade. We know that the four-fold occupational division of Bavra society existed much before Aryan way of living evolved. The two-fold Varnas of Rig-Vedic era that referred to Aryans and Dasas and the two-fold Jati division of Aryans and Bavras of Avestan world were the developments of later days, because Aryans came into existence much later, when evolved agriculture and trade.

However, it will be interesting to observe who all could have been the takers of the newly evolved professions of agriculture and trade. Bavra world had four-fold caste structure. Priestly class was called – Athornan. They were the religious teachers of society. They were looked upon with regards. They were spiritual guides of common men and all kinds of rites and rituals were conducted strictly under their supervision. They were considered demi-Gods dwelling on this earth. They were not only content with their elated position in the social stratification but they were also busy in continuous process of learning, teaching and supervising religious ceremonies that were an essential phenomenon of day-to-day activities. They had no reason to opt for any other profession. Nor did they have any leisure to indulge in another occupation simultaneously.

Similarly, the Ratheshtrans or Charioteers, who were called 'Kshatriyas' in later Avestan texts, comprised of the second caste in the hierarchy of social strata. They were people always engaged in defending territories. They were the warrior class. Even they were assigned the responsibility of immense social importance. They were the protectors as well as the rulers of land. It would have been very unusual on their part if they ever thought of changing their vocation. It would have been ridiculous and impractical. The last in the hierarchical ladder were Hutokshans. We are told they were artisans and labourers. They provided essential utensils and implements that were required in society. In those days, every thing was made or crafted by hand. This must have been an arduous and time taking job. Hutokshans must have been the lot that was always pressed hard to meet the requirements of Bavra world. Variety of things was needed in society. Utensils, bow, arrow, spear, axe, beads, ornaments, pottery and other such implements were required by almost every one. The list is inexhaustible. Hutokshans must have been some kind of man-machine – ever pressed hard to fulfill social demands. Even they could not be the likely takers of newly evolved occupation.

This leaves us with only Vashtaryoshins – the caste that came third in the echelon of social hierarchy. They were called Vaishya in Vedic civilization. Vashtaryoshins or Vaishyas were people whose occupation was agriculture, trade and rearing of cattle. But this social stratification of Bavra society preceded the advent of agriculture and trade. Agriculture evolved at a later stage. We may not rule out that some kind of trade of rudimentary nature might have existed in forest-dwelling societies of ancient world. But it could not have been of such a magnitude so as to involve a sizeable number of any clan or tribe. Safety and food stock was of prime importance in tribal world. Procurement of natural food for subsistence was an arduous task. It kept them busy all through out. They neither had much to trade nor any leisure for designing or producing new artifacts. But things changed with the knowledge of agriculture. From 'hunter-gatherer' they had themselves become the producers of food. The surplus availability of food stock freed them from daily routine of hunting and gathering. Cultivation did not necessitate continuous activities. It required seasonal involvement. Thus, men were not only freed from the dangers of daily hunting, they also had enough time to pursue other activities of their interest. No wonder we witness an accelerated process of evolution in all agro-based civilizations of this world. This heralded the beginning of full-fledged trade.

But what could have been the occupation of Vashtaryoshins in Bavra world? Could it be anything but cattle rearing? Yes. It was restricted to cattle-rearing alone. Agriculture and trade had not evolved till then. It is interesting to observe that in Avestan texts we come across the complete nomenclature of this caste. It was 'Vastaryoshin-pashuyanto'. Vashtaryoshin or Vaishya was the abridged form of Vashtaryoshin-pashuyanto. 'Pashu' is an Avestan as well as Sanskrit word for animals. 'Pashuyanto' definitely points out that this caste had something to do with cattle. In fact, cattle- rearing was the earliest occupation of mankind. Vashtaryoshin-Pashuyanto were people engaged in this profession. Now let us observe and compare their life-style with the remaining three castes of the Bavra world. These early Vashtaryoshins or Vaishyas used to take cattle to grazing grounds. There they spent almost entire day. They were bestowed with enough leisure time to spend hours in pastures. On the other hand, the same period would have been the busiest hours for the members of the remaining three castes. The remaining three were ever occupied in hunting, defenses, worshipping, performing or supervising rites and rituals to appease divinities and manufacturing implements of requirement. But Vashtaryoshin-pashuyanto were free to spend hours of daytime simply observing nature. They must have minutely observed the pattern of growth of plants in grazing pastures. They must have become familiar with cycle of growth and re-growth of different crops. They must have observed the factors that were responsible for better growth of different kinds of herbs and plants. They could have easily noticed the natural relationship of geography and its fauna. Indeed, these were the people, who had opportunity to experiment with flora and fauna of fertile pastures. Their wisdom had seeds that changed the shape of civilization. Gradually, their understanding of science of agriculture grew more. Thus, Vashtaryoshin-Pashuyanto must have been the earliest agriculturists. Men had learned the technique of easy production of surplus food. Their experimentation heralded a new era. Ways of living changed. This could have been the beginning of the process of Aryanisation.

Men moved to fertile lands that had natural irrigation facility. Villages and towns came up. The process of

Aryanisation was at full swing. But the members of remaining three castes must have been busy all throughout. They must have plunged into this wave of change at some later stage – to reap the harvest. Even after getting assimilated into this process of change, initially, their occupation remained unchanged. However, Vashtaryoshin-pashuyanto were the people who had acquired the knowledge of agriculture. They were the people who designed this new occupation. It was not too late to realize the potential of this new profession. Vashtaryoshin-pashuyanto switched over to this new occupation. Cattle-rearing became a thing of past. Vashtaryoshin-pashuyanto had become Vashtaryoshins or Vaishyas. 'Pashuyanto' was dropped off. Process of Aryanisation had begun with this change of occupation of Vaishyas. No wonder, at places, the term 'Vaishya' is rightly used in Vedic texts as the synonym of 'Arya'. Vashtaryoshins of Bavra world were the first Aryans. Phase of transition was set into motion.

Caste-system did not originate in Aryan world. It was not restricted to the Aryan society. Things become further clear as we analyse the evolution and meaning of caste-names. The group of people who were engaged in performance and supervision of rites and rituals for appeasement of divinities were considered the most important. In Aryan world they were called – Brahmans. But surprisingly, this priestly class was not called Brahman in pre-existing Bavra world. In Bavra society they were called – Athornans. We find it's corresponding identical in Vedic texts as well. In Vedic texts it was – Atharwan. Even in Vedic world, Atharwans were priests who supervised worship of Haoma and Agni (Fire). But why were Athornans or Atharwans not made the upper-most caste in Vedic world? It was there in the previous world too. Why Brahman – an altogether new name was attributed to this upper-most echelon of the hierarchical system? Were they any different from Athornans of Bavra society? If so, what was their chief occupation? What distinguished them from remaining three castes?

It is interesting to observe what different scholars have to say about Brahmanas. According to Manu-Smriti people engaged in performing following duties are called Brahmanas–

Adhyapanam adhyayanam yajanam yaajanam tatha
Danam pratigraham chaiwa braahmanaanaam kalpayat
(88 – Manu.)

It says – Brahmanas are people who engage in learning and teaching, performance and supervision of worships and who make, as well as accept donations. But according to other Smrities – 'Brahma jaanati Brahmanah' i.e. Brahmanas are people who possess divine perception or people who have knowledge of Almighty. However, Mahavira, the founder of Jainism, had somewhat different opinion. According to him people possessing certain essential virtues could only be considered Brahmanas. He further said – People who have the ability to lead life in a way that leads to the attainment of 'Moksha' and are capable of guiding others to attain the same are true Brahmans.

Bavra society was divided into four occupational castes. But besides this four-fold classification, the Bavras had one more type of people called 'Vohumanas'. 'Vohuman' literally means – 'the good mind'. Although, the Athornans were the priestly class yet, it was the Vohumanas who were accorded maximum respect in the Bavra society. Vohumanas were not restricted to any particular caste. It was initially a class in itself. It comprised of all those who were good- minded, pure at heart, saintly and benevolent to mankind – irrespective of caste. These Vohumanas kept on getting more and more importance in the society and by the time of Vedas they had attained the status of a distinct caste. With the passage of time, this Vohu-man became 'Bahman' or 'Brahman' in India and 'Behman' in Pazend language of Iran. Thus, in the beginning, Brahmans were not people belonging to a particular caste. They were the good-minded people of the society. They were Vohumanas.

In Vedic India, Athornan became Atharvan. It was no more a distinct class. Atharvans became a type of priests who were responsible for supervising the worship of fire (Agni) and Soma. The general priestly class had a new nomenclature – the Brahmans. It comprised of all 'vohumans'. And Atharvans got amalgamated in this new class. But this change was not easily comprehended and it appears that, throughout ancient days, the philosophers kept on trying to define who were Brahmans or Athornans. Early Zoroastrians had tried to define Athornans and while doing so, they made Vohumans out of them -

Him thou shall call an athravan,
who throughout the night sits up and demands of the holy wisdom,
which makes man free from anxiety,
with dilated heart, and cheerful at the head

In other words – the caste was not determined by birth. In the days of Zoroaster, it was the deeds of a man that decided whether he could be considered an Athornan. To be a Vohuman was the pre-requisite of an Athornan. These were the times when society was trying to make 'Vohumans' out of 'Athornans'. Thousands of years later, during the days of Buddha, we observe this process was almost complete. The Blessed One defines Brahmins as –

'Not by matted hair,
by clan, or by birth,

is one a Brahmin.
Whoever has truth & rectitude,
he is a pure one,
he, a Brahmin.'

And again he said –

'Whoever does no wrong
in body,
speech,
heart,
is restrained in these three ways.
he is what I call
a Brahmin.'

Thus, according to Buddha - only 'the Good Mind' (Vohumanas) could be considered a Brahmin.

It is interesting to observe that it was only the priestly class – Athornan or Brahman – that required detailed clarification, time and again. The philosophers of yesteryears did not feel the necessity of defining a new, the remaining three castes of the society. It is apparent that some kind of confusion was obviously existent about the first and foremost caste alone. In all probability, it was the magnetic field of all-important Vohumans that foreshadowed the Athornan class of early Indian society and by the time of Vedas, these Vohumans or Brahmans became the chief priestly class. Therefore, time and again, philosophers had to explain to the world the true purpose of this divine caste. Every time they tried to convey that 'the Good Mind' was ultimate and that caste was not determined by birth. As far as the remaining three castes were concerned, the caste identity remained solely based on parental lineage and occupation. Avestan texts reveal that when Ahura embarked upon creating this universe, in the beginning he created 'Vohu-Man'. According to Vedic mythology too, Almighty created

Brahmanas in the beginning. Avestan Vohumanas and Vedic Brahamans were no different.

Now, let us observe the developments that took place on Persian soil. The Avestan Vohuman became 'Behman' in Pazend language of Iran. In later Zoroastrian texts like 'Zend Avesta' we find this word 'Behman' used frequently. Everywhere it stands for 'Goodness' or 'the Good Mind'. Thus, the word had retained its original meaning in the ancient language of Iran. It could not become the new name of the foremost priestly caste there. This meaning of Behman had the potential to effectively impress upon the minds of the learned people. The Good Mind or the Behmans were revered since ages. We observe that in modern times, once again, a movement was started in Iran – based on the basic tenets of 'Behman'. The need to discard the multifarious sub- divisions of the society was strongly felt. Once again, it was felt that every kind of inequality had to be ignored. Once again, the saints of modern days had to reiterate that the only true means of salvation of mankind was the age old total 'Goodness' towards one and all; total 'Benevolence' towards one and all. This Behmanic movement of modern Iran was named 'the Behai' movement. Thus, literally, the 'Behai' movement of Iran is the age old 'Behmanic' or 'Brahmanic' movement that was intended to extol the virtues of 'Goodness' alone.

In ancient days, people were grouped in four-fold caste system chiefly on the basis of occupation. However, there still remained one of the most important occupations about which the caste system remains silent. We know that Fire and Soma were the two holiest things in the ancient Avestan and Vedic world. These were the only two earthly divinities. All religious rites and rituals centered on Soma (Haoma) and Fire. The later was considered as the son of 'Ahura' himself whereas Soma was the divine nector. Persons who were engaged in worshiping and supervising rituals of Fire and Soma constituted a distinct priestly class - the Athornans. In Bavra world, they comprised of the uppermost caste in social heirarchy. But we do not know anything about people who were engaged in making of Soma juice. We know it involved a complex and laborious process. Soma plants were available only on high mountain peaks. It was not easy to procure these plants. Great wisdom and effort must have been required to obtain Soma plants. The twigs were then crushed in stone mortars and juice thus obtained was filtered through seive. This complete process of making of Soma juice was, in itself, a riligious ritual of highest importance. 'Somadeva' - the God who looked after Soma plant - was worshipped to give good amount of Soma juice. Even the objects like stone mortar and seive were also worshipped. It was a long and tedious job. It involved skill at every step. At the same time, it was one of the holiest occupations of the ancient world. Therefore, we may conclude that there must have been a distinct group of individuals who were identified in society for being involved in this holiest occupation of mankind - that of making Soma-juice.

Since it involved great labour and skill, these people must have remained busy throughout to meet the daily social requirements of this holy nector. There is no reason why these people were not considered to constitute a distinct and important caste of their own. It was the holiest of all occupations. It involved making of divine nector. To consider these people as a distinct caste was so inevitable. Yet, ancient religious texts of Zoroastrians and Vedic people are silent about it. Could it be that, initially, Hutokshans were soma makers? Could it be that Hutokshans, in the beginning, were not artisans and labourers of the society? Avestan 'Hutokshan' could be corresponding identical of Sanskrit - 'Sutokshan'.

We know that 'Sut' in Sanskrit refers to Soma juice. Could it be that 'Sutokshan' or 'Hutokshan' were the people engaged in production of Soma juice? That seems quite rational.

We notice that the call-names designed for different occupational castes bear direct relation to the profession in which members of the particular caste were generally engaged. In Avesta, 'Fire' is called 'Athro'. Even in Veda, we are told that the sage 'Atharwa' was the first mortal who worshipped and created 'Fire'. The Vedic hymn says –

Atharva twa prathamo nirmanthagne[1]

Therefore, in those early days, the priestly class was named 'Athornan' or 'Atharvan'. They used to conduct and supervise the worship of 'Athro' i.e. 'fire'. This nomenclature of the priestly class had direct bearing to their occupation. We know how 'Vohu Manas' or the 'good mind' became 'Behmans' or 'Brahmans'. Similarly, earliest warriors in the society were called 'Ratheshtrans'. It was so because they used charriots (Ratha) for quick and easy maneuvers in battle. Initially, they just fought to defend their tribe or clan. It was the duty assigned to them. They were not the rulers of the land. In those days, the society was matriarchal and every thing was possessed and governed by 'Nairyo sangham'. But later on, when these warriors themselves became the rulers and the possessors of land, the nomenclature of the caste changed. In later Avestan texts and in Vedas, we find the name of this class as - 'Kshatriya'. 'Kshtra' is the Avestan as well as Sanskrit word for land, area, empire. Thus, 'Kshatriya' literally means the ruler of land. We know who all constituted 'Vashtaryoshin Pashuyanto'. Initially, their profession was cattle rearing. 'Pashuyanto' confirms it. We have seen how, later on, with the change of occupation, 'Pashuyanto' was dropped off and the

1 YajurVeda – Chapter – 11 – (32).

new name of the caste became - 'Vaishya'. These were the very first people who had indulged in the newly discovered profession of farming and trade. Thus, we find that the nomenclature of different classes had direct relation to the occupation in which they were engaged.

But 'Hutokshan' or 'Sutokshan', which later on became 'Shudra'in Vedic scriptures, does not bear any relation with the occupation that is believed to have been associated with this caste. Isn't that bewildering? The caste-name designed for this group must, in the like manner, bear a direct relation with the assigned occupation. It is so obvious. But the profession of artisans and labourers betrays any link with the caste-name designed for this group. 'Hutokshans' could not have been artisans and labourers. It is also true that, in early Bavra society, there could not be any room for artisans and labourers.These vocations must have been developments of later period. Concept of artisans and labourers before advent of agriculture is absurd. Tribal world had no use of labourers. Trade evolved at even later stage. But Bavra society existed prior to the advent of agriculture and it did have the class of people called - 'Hutokshans'. Therefore, 'Hutokshans' could be anything but artisans or labourers. In all probability, Hutokshans were initially 'Sutokshans' i.e. makers of Soma juice. 'Sutokshan' is a combined word. It is made up of two components – 'Sut' and 'ukshna'. 'Sut' literally means –'Soma'. 'Ukshna' means – to sprinkle, to squeeze out drop by drop. And that is exactly how elixir Haoma was obtained. The Haoma plants were crushed in stone mortars and pressed hard to squeeze out the elixir, which trickled down drop by drop. 'Hutokshan' or 'Sutokshan' could be nothing else. It could not be the general name of the caste or class of people comprising of labourers and artisans. We have another Sanskrit word – 'Sutwan'. Even 'Sutwan' literally means – the giver of Soma. Initially, 'Hutokshna' were people engaged in one of the most sacred professions of man kind – that of making the divine nector. When the process of Aryanization came in full swing, even Hutokshans migrated to the fertile plains. They had moved away from the terrain of Soma twigs. They could no more continue their old profession of making of Soma. Things were changing fast all around. Agriculture had changed the ancient style of living. Surplus production of food had brought in the concept of full-fledged trade and commerce. In this civilized agrarian world Hutokshans had no alternative but to induldge into some new lucrative profession. They became the labourers and artisans of Aryan world.

Making of the 'Divine Nector' (Haoma) was the distinct occupation of Hutokshans alone. This is also evident from the 'Yasnas' that are dedicated to Haoma. In Zoroastrian Gatha, Yasna – 9 to 11 are attributed to Haoma. In these 'Yasnas', we are told that the first three castes or classes of the society were not found in the land of Haoma (Soma). Observe the following hymn of Gatha –

nOiT ahmi nmAne zAnAite[1]
Aqrawa naEDa raqaEStI
naEDa WAstryO fCuy&s

'noit' stands for 'not'. 'ahmi' is 'mine'. 'nmane' can be translated as "home'. 'Zanaite' means – 'to be'. Here, the root word is – 'jan'. Even in Sanskrit, the word 'janyate' means the same. 'Aqrawa' (Athornan), 'raqaesti' (ratheshtran) and 'wastryo fcuy&s (vashtaryoshin pashuyanto) are the first three castes or classes of the social hierarchical classification. The hymn says –

(Thus said Haoma)In my place of residence you will not find Athornans, Ratheshtrans or Vashtaryoshin pashuyanto.

1 Gatha – Yasna – 11 – para – (6).

This leaves 'Hutokshans' alone. It confirms our view. We were right in concluding that 'Hutokshans' could be 'Sutokshans', who were engaged in the preparation of 'Haoma' elixir. In fact, they were the only people in Bavra world, who knew where Haoma plants grew. They were the only people, who treaded the land of Haoma. They were the people who fetched Haoma twigs. They were ever engaged in crushing, extracting and filtering of the Divine Nector. Thus, initially, Hutokshans were people engaged in one of the holiest occupation of mankind. Haoma and Fire were the most important worldly deities of ancient world. Preparation of Divine Nector would have been the most sacred profession of Bavra world. It could have been as sacred as the occupation of 'fire-worship'. But things changed with advent of agriculture and trade.

This four-fold occupational division of society was fully developed in pre-Aryan Bavra world. But it did not constitute four distinct 'Jatis' in Avestan world. They are nowhere referred to as distinct Jati in Zoroastrian texts. In Bavra world, the term 'Jati' was used to differentiate Aryans from Bavras i.e. Non-Aryans. Bavra was a 'Jati' in Avestan society. And so was 'Arya'. There were just two 'Jatis' in Zoroastrian world. When process of Aryanization began, this four-fold system of occupational classification was assimilated in Aryan world too. But even in Rig-Veda, this did not constitute four distinct 'Varnas'. Initially, Varna- vyawastha of Rig-Veda was two-fold system of classification. It was corresponding identical of 'Jati-vyawastha' of pre-existing Bavra world. Varna-vyawastha of Rig-Veda and Jati-vyawastha of Bavra world remained a two-fold system of classification – segregating Aryan way of living from non-Aryan way of living. 'Varna' and Jati' were synonyms till early Vedic days.

However, with the passage of time, further sub-divisions or classifications came into effect that gave rise to distinctly identifiable groups within Aryan community. They could be distinguished from each other chiefly on the basis of occupation. 'Jati', in its real sense, is not used in Rig-Veda. Yet we find many occupational groups that are, in Rig-Veda, easily identifiable as constituting different 'Jati'. In later Vedic texts they are, indeed, considered as distinct 'Jati'. They were – 'Vapta' or barber, 'Tashta' or carpenter, 'Bhishak' or practitioner of medicine, 'Charman' or chamar, and 'Karmar' or blacksmith. It shows that, even during early Rig-Vedic days, many specialized occupations had evolved and that people engaged in these trades were granted distinct identity in the society. However, in early Vedic days, they were not called or considered as different 'Varna' or 'Jati'. But in later period, each such group was believed to constitute a distinct 'Jati'. It appears that, by this time, the term 'Jati' was incorporated in Vedic texts. Use of 'Varna' was restricted only for four-fold classification system that had been pre-existing even in Bavra world. And 'Jati' was used, in general, for all further divisions and sub-divisions. This is, in general, the relation between 'Varna' and 'Jati'. Initially, Vedic 'Varna' was corresponding identical of Avestan 'Jati'. Both were two-fold classification system. However, with passage of time, the four – fold occupational classification of ancient Bavra socity, which had got incorporated in Vedic world too, was called the four Varnas. 'Jati' – which was initially the technical Avestan word for differentiation between Aryans and Non-Aryans, got place in later Vedic scriptures, where it was applied to all further sub-divisions of social groups.

NAIRYO – SANGHAM

Mubad Nairyosangh Daval aedar yad bad[1]

This is a line from Khordeh Avesta. It says – 'Mobed Nairyosangh Daval be remembered here'. It is in Pazend language. These were times when 'Nairyosangh' had become proper name of some individual. But, in the days of Avesta, it had a different meaning altogether. Let us get into the past.

Neolithic civilization of Indo-Iranian terrain witnessed the advent of agriculture. It was a transition of immense magnitude. In preceding era, man was a 'hunter-gatherer'. Now, he produced food himself. Earlier, his style of living was different. He was always on the move. Fresh pastures were required for his domesticated animals. Fresh hunting grounds were sought after to meet his daily requirement of food. He could stick to a particular area only as long as it could naturally support him. Hunting necessitated that they lived together – in groups. Thus, the first social unit that must have come into existence was this group or band. It consisted of an extended family whose members had matrilineal relations. Those days, relations could only be matrilineal because they had no concept of marriage. They fought and defended together. They hunted together. The food thus obtained belonged to all members. They never existed individually. They could not. Safety measures required that they existed in the form of a formidable band or group. Initially, the female members of this band or clan could have been participating in the activities of hunting and fighting to defend. But their long spells of pregnancies and their natural involvement in

1 Khordeh Avesta – Prayer for remembering the dead.

rearing of newborns would have resulted in their frequent absence from the hunting ground. One cannot rule out that some of them, who were free to accompany, might have been taking part in their daily fight for existence but, by and large, a significant number of them always had to stay behind at some safe base-camp. Gradually, this base-camp would have become the nucleus of the band. Each morning the male-members would fan out in search of food. Each evening they would fall back to this base-camp – to eat, to rest and to recuperate. In ancient days, this base camp was called 'Nairyo Sangh'. It was the place which housed congregation of the female members of 'hunter-gatherers'.

But advent of agriculture changed the ancient way of living. Agriculture required fertile lands with easy irrigation facilities. Men started living in open fields – away from jungles. They were no more dependent on forests that provided animals for hunting. They were no more dependent on food that could be procured from it. Rather, they had themselves become producers of food. They started settling on riverbanks. Earlier, they preferred living in the vicinity of forests or foothills. This change of habitat had profound importance in the later course of civilization. Agriculture freed them, gradually, from the compulsion of community living. Men were free to live individually. Life in open fields was secure and easy. This resulted in gradual individualistic set-up in that era. For the first time men started building their own individual houses and the concept of individual family came into existence. It was an important step of civilizations world over. It changed the ancient understanding of relationship. But, in ancient days, kinship was established only through the base-camp or the nucleus of tribes that consisted of female members. This base-camp gave them sons and daughters. It gave them identity. The inter-clan or inter-tribal relations could also be worked out only through affiliations to this core female body. This core female body was looked upon with veneration in society. Gradually, it became a sacred institution. We may presume that this core female body was the first temple that came into existence in this world. But agriculture brought in an unprecedented upheaval. The female pre-dominance was replaced by male pre-dominance. However, Avestan society still revolved around matrilineal relations. Observe the following line of Khordeh Avesta –

Nairim sanghem yazamaide[1]

In the same text, it is translated as – 'the valliant commandments are revered'. But, at another place in the same text, we find its given explaination somewhat different. Observe the same line in Atash Niyaish of Khordeh Avesta–

Nairyo Sanghahe yazatahe[2]

Here, in Atash Niyaish, it is translated as – 'the progeny of rulers, of brave principles'. I don't know why things are explained so erroneously. We know that 'Nairyo' is the Avestan as well as Sanskrit word for 'women'. 'Sangham' is yet another word common in both languages. It stands for 'monastery', 'congregation', 'institution', 'vihara' or 'matha'. 'Yazamaide' is as usual – 'yazam ide'. Thus the line can be translated as – 'We revere, hereby, the monastery of females'.

It is interesting to observe that there never existed something like 'Naram sangham', which could have been corresponding similar institution of male members of the society. There is not a single occasion in the entire Avestan texts, which refers to any such monastery or institution of men. It was just not there. This 'Nairyo sangham' was the nucleus of the Avestan society. At places, it is eulogized just

1 Khordeh Avesta – Havan Geh – para (9)

2 Khordeh Avesta – Atash Niyaish – para – (10).

as other divinities are. It proves that this 'body of females' had attained so much importance in the society that it was granted some kind of divine status. Also, it is one of the distinguishing features of the Zoroastrian liturgical texts. But Vedic civilization was male predominant. And we have an almost clear picture of the cultural and social upheavals that followed in this country since Vedic period. Nowhere do we get the slightest hint of a society that is female predominant; a society that is matriarchal. This leaves us with no choice. Avestan philosophy was pre- Vedic. Avestan people lived any time before our Vedas were compiled.

In the days of Gatha, Gods were worshipped to bless with daughters. Observe the following Avestan hymn, which is dedicated to Haoma –

DaD&mi im&m tanUm[1]
YA mE WaEnaite huraOda

'Dadmi' is – to give. Here, the root word is – 'da'. It is identically found in Sanskrit as well. Even in Sanskrit the word 'Dadami' means just the same. Like Sanskrit, even Avestan word 'im&m' stands for – here, like this. 'TanUm' is found in Sanskrit as well. It stands for – progeny, offspring. In Sanskrit the words 'Tanuj' and 'Tanuja' stand for 'son' and 'daughter'respectively. In Avesta, as well as in Sanskrit, the meaning of 'Ya' is – who. Similarly, in both languages, 'mE' is – me. The root word in 'WaEnaite' is 'Ni'. It is identically found in Sanskrit as well. Avestan word 'WaEnaite'can be translated as – to bring, to produce. Even in Sanskrit – Anayati – has exactly similar meaning. Avestan 'huraOda' is – daughters. Thus, the aforesaid hymn can be translated as-

(O Haoma!) give us here such offsprings
Who bring to us – daughters.

1 Gatha – Yasna – 10 – para – (14).

In the days of Zoroaster, only daughters were important. And so was the 'Nairyo Sangham'.

In all probability these 'Nairyo Sanghams' were the governing bodies of the ancient world. Observe the following lines of Khordeh Avesta (Havan Geh) -

Apam Naptarem yazamaide[1]
Nairim Sanghem yazamaide
Takhmam Damoish Upmanam yazatem yazamaide

It says – We, hereby, worship Apam Naptarem; we, hereby, worship the Nairyo Sangham; we, hereby, worship Taksha, who created this thunder like thing. Here, 'Nairyo-Sangh' is accorded divine status. We know that 'Apam-Naptarem' and 'Takhmem' (Taksha) are corresponding identicals of Vedic divinities'Apam-Napat' and 'Twashtra' respectively.

In Zoroastrian mythology, 'Nairyo-Sangh' was of immense importance. Even the identity of females was related with the particular 'Viharas of the Females' (Nairyo-Sangh) to which they belonged or where they were born and brought up. Observe the following lines of Avesta: -

Nairimcha Sanghem huraodhem[2]

It can be translated as – 'These daughters of the Nairyo-Sangham'. The daughters got their identity from the 'Nairyo-Sangham' to which they belonged. Thus, Avestan world was definitely matriarchal. These female bodies governed the society and the identity of females was related with these institutions. We do not get any description of the sons of Nairyo Sangham. On the other hand we have references where Lord Ahura is worshipped to bless with daughters: -

---

1 Khordeh Avesta – Havan Geh – para (9).
2 Khordeh Avesta – Sarosh Yasht Vadi – para – (34).

DAyI-Me ahurAne ahurahe nairy&m Asn&m frazaNtIm[1]
YA Me frADayAT nmAnvmca WIsvmca ZaNtUmca dafyUmca

The first line of this hymn is addressed to Lord Ahura. Here, God Ahura is worshipped to bless with daughters. The hymn further says that it is women who provide us the home, the village and the town. The hymn proves that the law of inheritance in the matriarchal society went down the chain of daughters only. Thus, it was only females who owned everything – the house was theirs, the village was theirs, the town was theirs. It was through them and because of them that men identified their village, township or relations. 'YA Me frADayAT' stands for – 'who give to us'. We know that 'nmAnvm', 'WIsvm' and 'ZaNtUm' are home, village and town respectively. Nairyo Sangham was, in those days, of immense social importance and its divine status was absolutely justified. Now observe the following line of 'Atash Niyaish' of Khordeh Avesta-

khshathro nafedhro Nairyo Sangahe yazatahe[2]

'khshathro' i.e. kshatro means 'land', 'empire', 'area'. 'Nafedhro' is the corresponding identical of 'naptri'. It stands for – 'grand sons/daughters'. 'Nairyo Sangahe' is 'Nairyo-Sangh'. In 'yazatahe' the root word is – 'yaj'. It can be translated as – an act of worship or reverence. The hymn says –

We worship the country of grand sons and
daughters of Nairyo Sangh.

Or

We worship the land which is inhabited by the grand sons
and daughters of Nairyo Sangh.

---

1 Gatha – Yasna – 68 – para – (5).

2 Khordeh Avesta – Atash Niyaesh – para – (10).

People, in those early days, got their identity through Nairyo Sangh alone. Nairyo Sangh was the nucleus of society. It was the governing body. This Avestan hymn is a eulogy offered to the land of Nairyo Sangh. Ancient Avesta speaking Iranians knew the place from where they had originated. They knew that their home-land was located deep inside Amavant, where existed Bavra society, where lived the grand sons and daughters of Nairyo Sangh.

Another change that can be perceived in agro-based civilizations of Indo-Iranian domain is the veneration of the Bull. Cow was worshipped in the ancient world. It was because of the utility value of the cow. Men have consumed milk and milk-products since very old days. Cow was an easy source of readymade food. It did not involve any precarious journey into forests that the 'hunter-gatherer' had to undertake to subsist himself. Domestication of cow would have been so relieving to them. Whenever they could not carry out hunting or gathering of food, they could easily fall back to its nutritious milk for their subsistence. Later, when agriculture became the way of living, the importance of cow grew even further. It provided ox for ploughing fields. Cow-dung was the first manure that man used for cultivation. The importance of cow was immense. No wonder, in ancient days, cow was considered to be the token of wealth. The number of cows possessed decided the status of an individual. Gradually, an aura of divinity was attached to the cow. It was considered sacred. People of ancient days started worshipping the cow. Things remained so till the time men took to agriculture. It was from here on that the importance of bull was recognized in the society. The bull was employed to plough fields. Thus, in agro-based civilizations of Indo-Iranian terrain, we observe a shift of attitude. For the first time, we find that even the bull is accorded a divine status. The people of Indus valley worshipped bull. This cult of bull-worship can also be observed in the civilizations that flourished in the fertile lands of Euphrates and Tigris.

But veneration of cow is an older tradition. Avestan people had, in the beginning, not opted for newly evolved profession of agriculture and trade. They preferred to continue with their tribal way of living. And they continued their age old practice of worshipping cows. Observe the following hymn of Yasna 29 of the Avestan Gatha –

YUZVm aEiByO ahurA aogO data[1]

It can be translated as – 'you Ahura, are the giver of cows'. Here, the word 'gao-O' has been erroneously transcribed as – 'aog-O'.

We find many occasions where some of the words are erroneously transcribed in Gatha. There is yet another Avestan passage –

Gave nemo, gave nemo,[2]
Gave uxdem, gave verethrem,
Gave xarethem, gave vastrem,
Gave verezyatem,

Its word-byword meaning is as follows –

Gave	–	cow
Nemo	–	worship
Uxdem	–	pray
Verethrem	–	(from root Vri) to protect
Xarethem	–	to feed
Vastrem	–	to provide shelter
Verezyatem	–	husbandry, to work

1 Gatha – Yasna – 29 – para – (10).

2 Gatha – Yasna – 10 (Haoma Yasht) - para – (20).

Thus, the whole thing can be translated as – 'One should worship the cow, offer prayers to the cow, always readily protect the cow, put sincere efforts to feed and provide shelter to the cow and thus remain ever willing for cow – rearing'.

Does it not indicate that Avestan society existed much before Indus valley civilization? Indus Valley civilization was the earliest agro-based civilization. It dates back to roughly fifth millennium BC. Does it not indicate that the Zoroastrian saga refers to events that took place any time before fifth millennium BC? Yes. Even Zoroaster's world was matriarchal. But it did not precede the patriarchal male pre-dominant agricultural society. Rather, it co-existed with latter. It will be fair to presume that Zoroaster was born in an era of transition. It was a period of transition from forest dwelling to agriculture. It was the era of change of habitat from forest-centric to river-centric. It was the phase of transition of life-style. However, on this subject, there is an interesting hymn in Gatha –

AiryamanascA nadvaNtO gVuScA[1]

It says – even Aryans worship cows. In all probability, the age-old practice of cow worship was not lost in the newly evolved Aryan society. Thus, we may conclude that, alongwith bull worship, the practice of cow worship also continued in Aryan world.

We have seen earlier that Aryans and Zoroaster lived together harmoniously. The Avestan hymns proclaim that Aryans were people with perpetual doubts. They often invited Zoroaster for clarification of doubts. When Zoroastrians declared that Aryans were people having perpetual doubts, they, indirectly, also revealed the existence of at least one more class of people from whom these Aryans could be

1 Gatha – Yasna – 33 – para – (4).

distinguished because of this peculiar trait of theirs. Aryans were characterized by incessant doubts. It presupposes existence of another lot, which lacked this peculiarity. Aryans were called so because there existed another class of people, who were, comparatively, better endowed with religious wisdom. Their conviction had more strength. They were not hounded by incessant doubts. Also, one may conclude, from the way things are expressed, that even Zoroaster belonged to the other lot. We often get the mention of 'barvasmanai cha' in Avestan texts. It can be translated as – 'The Bavra people too'. 'Barvasmanai' is a compound word. It is made up of two components – 'Barva'(Bavra) and 'Manai'. 'Manai' is the Sanskrit as well as Avestan word for 'people'. Thus 'Barvasmanai' is - the Bavra people. It is evident from this Avestan reference that the two groups co-inhabiting roughly around fifth millennium B.C. in this part of the world, were the Aryans and the Bavras.

But history teaches us that invading Aryans came from steppes of Eurasia. They defeated 'Dasas' – who were natives of this place and who were racially different. Strangely enough, in Vedic texts, we come across passages that contradict this idea. Things become clear when we come across the following prayer of Rig Vedic hymn that is addressed to Indra –

'We prey you to give us enough wealth so that we can make Aryans out of Dasas.'

Now, that is a wonderful piece of information. It suggests that by means of wealth alone Vedic Aryans could possibly change or convert Dasas into Aryans. But how could that be? If they were two different races – then all worlds' treasures put together could not do much. A race is determined only by birth. Nothing can change it. But Vedic hymn suggests that it was possible. In that case we aren't left with much choice. We will have to take it for granted that it was not the divide based on racial difference. Aryans could be made out of Dasas because Aryans and Dasas were of the same race. Their differentiation was based on ways of living. People who adopted civilized ways of living were called Aryans. 'Arya' literally means 'civilized' or 'educated'. Dasas, who were called Bavras in Avestan texts, were people who preferred their primitive ways of living. 'Bavra' is a Sanskrit word. It means uneducated, uncivilized, tribal or living in forests. 'Bavra' is the antonym of 'Arya'. Bavras were people who had still not taken to agricultural life. They still preferred living like nomadic hunters. Thus, it was quite possible for Vedic Aryans to try and make more Aryans out of Dasas or Bavras by educating them and by providing them means of livelihood that could change their ways of living. All this required enough wealth and that was the reason Lord Indra was worshipped to provide treasures to make Aryans out of Dasas.

Aryans and Bavras lived together during the days of Zoroaster. To which group did the Prophet belong? Observe the following line -

Zaotra haDA barvasma Ayese Yesti[1]

It says - 'by caste (we are) bavra. So it is.' Avestan 'Zaotra' is the corresponding identical of Sanskrit – 'zetri', which stands for – caste. 'HaDA' stands for – is, to be. 'Aise yesti' is identically found in Sanskrit as well. It can be translated as – so it is. Now observe the next line -

Barvasm haDa zaotra Ayese Yesti[2]

It says - 'because we are bavra, that is our cast. So it is.' This line almost confirms that Bavra was definitely a way of living and this special way of living had the essence of difference that determined their caste. Thus, Zoroastrianism

1 Gatha – Yasna – 2 – para (1).

2 Gatha – yasna – 2 – para – (1).

was basically the Bavra religion and the Prophet was the philosopher of the Bavra world. However, if we consider that the era of Zoroaster was the period of transition from Bavra way of living to Aryan way of living and that, in the days of Zoroaster, both Bavras and Aryans co-existed, then we must get some reference of it in Vedas as well. Avestan texts clearly present before us a society where people were divided into Arya and Bavra. If Avestan texts admit the existence of Aryan people then we ought to get the reference of Bavra people in the Vedas too. Observe what Sam Veda has to say about Bavra people –

Tawahmo som raran sakyaitye divedive[1]
Puruni bavro ni charanti mamav paridhi rati tan ih

The line has been translated as – 'Soma! Let me have the blessing of your friendship. Many types of wicked people are causing inconvenience to me. Destroy them.'

Here the word 'Bavra' has been explained as 'a group of wicked people'. But 'Bavra' is a pure Sanskrit word. It stands for tribal, non-Aryan or uncivilized. Here, the use of Bavra distinctly refers to a distinct group of people, who were ancient inhabitants of this country. It does not refer to 'wicked people' in general. Observe that 'Bavro' is preceded by the adjective – 'Puruni'. 'Puruni' is an Avestan as well as a Sanskrit word for – 'old or ancient'. 'Puruni bavro' exactly means – the ancient Bavra people. There is no other occasion in entire Vedic literature where 'Bavra' is used to express – wicked persons. 'Puruni Bavro' is nothing else but – the ancient Bavra people. The truth is that Vedic hymns were compiled long time ago. It was only after lapse of more than thousand years that some efforts were made by Indian scholars to translate Vedic hymns in languages that could be understood easily

1 Sam Veda – (516).

by common men. By that time, it had become quite difficult to understand many of the archaic Vedic words. The word 'Bavra' cannot mean 'wicked people'. Avestan texts make it obviously clear that 'Bavra' was a distinct class of people. It says that Aryans and Bavras lived together happily, during those early days, when the profession of agriculture and trade had just heralded. Also, the expression – 'puruni Bavro' makes it obviously clear that the Bavra way of living preceded the Aryan way of living. There remains no doubt whatsoever. Now observe the following hymn of Rig-Veda –

Yadim soma babhrudhuta[1]

Here, the word 'babhru-dhuta' has been explained by Swamy Dayanand Saraswati as – 'purified by the learned sages'. Bavru people were not only respected in Aryan society, they were also known for producing, purifying and consecrating the Divine Nector (Soma). Similarly, there is another hymn in Rig-Veda that says –

Bavru yameshu shobhate[2]

In his translations of Rig-Veda, Swamy Dayanand Saraswati has explained this word 'Bavru' as – teacher or preacher. Thus 'Bavru yameshu shobhate', according to him, means – 'Bavra people add grace to all occasions'. Now observe the following hymn of Rig-Veda –

Pururupa ugro babhruh[3]

'Pururupa' is – ancient. 'Ugro' means – violent. The hymn says –

The ancient Bavra people, who are violent in nature

---

1 RigVeda – Ashtak (4) – Adhyay (1) – Varg (28).

2 Rig Veda – Ashtak (3) – Adhyay (6) – Varg (26).

3 Rig Veda – 2 – 4 – (33).

Isn't it exactly similar to the earlier hymn of Sam-Veda? 'Puruni' Bavra people are addressed here as – 'Puru rupa' Bavra people. At both places, it exactly means – the ancient Bavra people. These Vedic hymns clearly indicate that Bavra way of living preceded Aryan way of living. In the days of Zoroaster two distinct cultures flourished simultaneously. There were two different worlds – one was called Aryan and the other Bavra. But in those days, the phase of transition was set into motion. Agriculture had ushered new way of living. Those who became associated with the emerging new world were called Aryans. Those who preferred to stick to traditional way of living were called Bavrasmanas, Bavru, Briwi, Bratya or Dasa.

'Brahamanas' are the religious texts that constitute an essential part of Vedic literature and some of them are considered as old as the Vedas themselves. 'Tandya Brahman' is considered to be one of the earliest. It gives a very interesting description of conversion of Bratyas into Aryans. And while doing so, it clearly lays down the characteristics of Bratyas. According to Tandya Brahman, Bratyas could be distinguished on two main grounds. Firstly, Bratyas were people who did not undertake agriculture or trade as their basic occupation. Secondly, although they did not follow the essential rites and rituals of Aryans, they could not be differentiated on grounds of their speech. These Bratyas of 'Tandya Brahman' are none other than the ancient Bavra people.This description of 'Tandya Brahman', again, makes it obviously clear that both Aryans and Bratyas were people from the same part of the world. They were of same race. They spoke same language. The only thing that differentiated them was their ways of living. Aryans were people who had taken to agriculture and trade. Bratyas had not. Bratyas preferred their ancient ways of living. In 'Tandya Brahman' Bavras are called - Bratyas.

And, according to 'Tandya Brahman', it was quite possible to convert Bratyas into Aryans. The process to be followed is described in detail in the 'Brahaman'. It again proves that Bratyas were not of different race. You are never converted to a race. You are born to it. These Bratyas were none other than Bavras of Avesta.

However, later-Vedic literature and 'meemansha-shashtra' tries to define Bratyas somewhat differently. It was believed that a Bratya had to perform sacrifice by way of – 'Bratyashtoma' before he could be accepted as an Aryan. Meemansha-shashtra defines Bratyas as men and women from the three higher castes who lost the taste of Soma for three generations. It says that people whose father, grandfather and great-grandfather abstained from taking Soma juice were called Bratyas. To condone this ineligibility, they were required to sacrifice an extra goat in the religious sacrifice. On the other hand, in the commentary of Namakbhashya, Vidyaranya defines 'Bratebhyah' as 'nana jati sanjatah' i.e. born to various groups of people. But another commentator – 'Bhattabhashkara' said that Bratyas were people who had no definite way of living and that they constituted of all the castes. It clearly depicts the kind of confusion that surrounds the meaning of Bratya. Thousands of years had lapsed between the existence of Bavras or Bratyas and compilation of later-Vedic literature. People had lost track. Different scholars explained Bratyas differently. They were ignorant of Bavra culture. An ancient civilization was lost to them.

However, in the pre-Aryan world of Bavras, God Indra was non-existent. We do not have a single reference to God Indra in entire seventy-two chapters of Zoroastrian Gatha. Vedic Indra is the God of Rain and Thunder. The importance of rain is significantly associated with cultivation of crops. Prior to the advent of agriculture, rain must have been an occasional, unwelcome and unimportant phenomenon. In ancient days, the 'hunter-gatherers' must have become uncomfortable during rainy seasons. It would have disturbed their daily routine of hunting and food gathering. Even if they had assigned some name to the deity who looked after rain, they had no reason to replace the old all-important Sun God or Ahura with the God of Rain. The significance of rain grew only after the advent of agriculture. Thus, the importance of Rain God can be reasonably linked with the process of Aryanization. Indra – the God of Rain – definitely belongs to the world of Aryans. He was the most important divinity of Vedic civilization. He is considered mightiest of all Vedic deities. 'Rig Veda' has maximum number of hymns in his praise.

Rig-Vedic society practiced agriculture and worshipped Indra – the Rain God. In Vedic hymns, Indra was also called 'Vritraghna'. It was so because, as the Hindu mythology goes, he had slain the demon – 'Vritra'. The hymns of Rig Veda describe how Indra killed Vritra, by means of his famous thunder like weapon- 'Vajra'. It further narrates how, after the death of 'Vritra', thousands of cows came running out of the caves, where they were kept in captivity. 'ghna' is a suffix, which means 'to kill'. That is how Indra was named 'Vritraghna' - the slayer of the demon Vritra. But we have another 'Veretraghna' too. In Avestan texts, even Lord Ahura is named so. And he is called so for a different reason. Here the meaning of the word 'Veretra' i.e. 'Vritra' is 'darkness'. 'Vritra' is also the Sanskrit word for darkness. Ahura is named so because he removes or kills darkness and shows light to the mankind. Strange! The same epithet is used for both! We know that all Avestan divinities are Vedic too. Both philosophies evolved on Indian soil. You just cannot differentiate between them. Yet, Indra is not there in Zoroastrian Gatha. It proves, beyond doubt, that the philosophy of Gatha is pre- Indra. Gatha pertains to the civilization that existed prior to the advent of agriculture. However, in later Avestan texts, we do get the mention of God Indra. Observe the following line of Vendidad –

daEwan&m daEwO iNdrO daEwO[1]

Compared to Gatha, Vendidad is of much later period. It proves that God Indra was not there in the Bavra world. God Indra evolved much later, in the world of Aryans. But when did that happen? When did Indra come into existence? Of course we are not sure of that. But one thing is clear. Indra was the God of agrarian society and, by around later half of third millennium B.C., Indra was already established as the most important Aryan divinity.

We get written record of his name in 'Boghaj- koi' inscriptions that dates back to 1400 B.C. 'In-di- ra' is the first name inscribed on it, followed by the names of other deities. It goes like this –

In-di-ra
Mi- it- ra
Uru-wa-na
Na-sa-tya

The mention of 'In-di-ra' in Boghaz Koi inscriptions confirms that Indra was already there in Indo-Aryan mythology in around fourteenth century B.C. Also, the mention of his name in the first place suggests that, by that time, he had attained the most significant status among the divinities of Aryan mythology. In Vedic religion he was considered to be the king of all deities. He was the most valiant and powerful of all Gods in the pantheon of mythological divinities of Indo-Aryans.

---

1 Vendidad – Chapter – 19 – para – (43).

But let us have a re-look at this inscription found in Boghaz Koi. 'Varuna's' absence here is more significant. Varuna is an important Vedic deity, whose name is invariably paired with 'Mitra'. Through out Vedic texts, Mitra-Varuna paired together, come innumerable times. There seems to be some kind of relation-ship between the two, but it is not clear anywhere. Even later Vedic literature is silent about it. There neither appears any correlation in the power and function assigned to them. Still, Vedic people had some reason to pair them together. Things get further mixed up when we notice another deity - 'Mitravarun' in the Vedic texts. There could be, probably, two schools of thoughts. One was satisfied with the paired expression of the two deities whereas the other thought of 'Mitravarun' as a single divinity. But in the aforesaid Boghaz Koi inscriptions Mitra is mentioned without Varuna. And that is strange.

In all probability, Vedic 'Varuna' was the God of the Winds. At some places he is also considered as 'The Lord of the Seas'. We have occasions where Varuna is considered to be 'The God of the Night Sky' because he is invariably paired with 'Mithra', who is the 'God of Day Light'. This Vedic 'Varuna' has distinctly identifiable corresponding similar divinity in other civilizations as well. Greeks called him – 'Uranus'. Slavic people called him – 'Velos' and Lithuanians called him – 'Velorias'. But what was he called in Zoroastrian religion? It is strange. He is just not there in earliest hymns. Like Indra, even Varuna is not there in Avestan Gatha. Even Varuna evolved at much later stage. We get the mention of Varuna only in Zoroastrian religious texts that were compiled much later. Observe what is said about Varuna in Greater Bundahishna –

'The dev Varun is that which practices unnatural lust.[1]
One says – The Varun without the path.'

Greater Bundahishna came into existence almost two thousand years after Gatha. Varuna is not there in earliest Avestan hymns. Bavra civilization neither had Indra nor Varuna. However, in the aforesaid Boghaz Koi inscription, Mithra is followed by 'Uru-wa-na'. Isn't that almost close to – Varuna?

In all probability, this 'Uru-wa-na' was the proto-type of Vedic 'Varuna' and Greek 'Uranus'. Its origin can be fairly traced back to Avestan saga. All had originated from the same stalk. 'Uru-wa-na' too, had its origin in Avestan world. In Avestan religious texts, Mithra is invariably followed by – 'wo-uru'. Observe the following hymn of Yasna 2 of Gatha –

Miqrvm Wouru-gaoyaoitIm[2]

It says – Mitra, the lord of cows. This 'wo-uru' of Avestan Gatha evolved to become 'Wo-uru-na' i.e. Varuna of Vedic mythology. However, as it proceeded further north and west, 'wo-uru' became, in all probability, 'uru-wa' and 'uru-wa-na'. This 'uru-wa-na' became 'Uranus' in Greek mythology. It is interesting to observe that in Greek, the name 'Uranus' was, in olden days, pronounced as – 'Ouranos'. It also explains the reason of pairing of the two divinities Mitra and Varuna, in the Vedas. Vedic Varuna was a well-defined deity. It was not necessary to pair him with some other divinity. He could have been invoked individually. But, almost throughout Vedic texts, he is paired with – Mitra. That reveals the link. People had a notion of his origin. They knew that he was somehow related to Mitra. Some of them preferred pairing them together where as the other school considered that Mitravarun had to

---

1 Greater Bundahishna – Chapter – XXVII – (30).
2 Gatha – Yasna – 2 – para – (3).

be a single divinity as 'Mitra wouru gaoyao' had been. It is interesting to observe that, according to Yajur Veda (Chapter – VII - 10), Mitravarun was the giver of cows.

But let us come back to Zoroastrian Gatha. In Avesta, Mitra is considered as the keeper of cows. Observe the following lines where 'Mitra' is being worshiped and invited –

Mithrahe wourugaoyaotoish hazanghro-gaoshahe baivarechashmano[1]
aoktho namno yazatahe ramano khastrahe

The meaning of each word is given below –

Mithrahe	- Mithra
Wourugaoyaotoish	- Lord of cows
Hazanghra-gaoshahe	- With thousand ears
Baivarechashmano	- With ten thousand eyes
Aokhto	- Invite
Namno	- In the house
Yazatahe	- Worship
Ramno khastrahe	- In this country of Rama (or in this good land)

The line can be translated as – 'Mithra, the Lord of cows, is bestowed with thousand ears and ten thousand eyes. In this country of Rama (or in this good land), we worship him and invite him to our houses'. Throughout Avestan texts Mitra is invariably expressed as 'Mitra wouru gaoyaoitIm', which exactly means ' Mitra, the lord of cows'. There is a remarkably similar line in Vedas as well –

Mitravaruna ghritairgavyuti[2]

1 Khordeh Avesta – Havan Geh – para – (2).
2 Sam Veda – (220).

This Vedic hymn prays the deity 'Mitravarun' to make the milk of the cow creamier. 'Ghritai' is 'cream' of milk. If this word is removed from the aforesaid line we will be left with 'mitravaruna gavyuti', which is so identical to 'mitra wo-uru gaoyoitim' of Avestan texts.

Things were changing fast all around. A well settled agrarian society had come up in the Sapt-Sindhu regeion. The age old living style of Bavra world was fading to oblivion. Agriculture and trade had gradually become the new profession of mankind. New deities evolved and 'Indra'- the God of rain – had become the most important divinity. It is interesting to observe that each and every Avestan divinity is incorporated in Vedic religion but Vedic religion has many divinities that are just not there in Bavra religion. Does it not indicate that the foundation of this newly evolving religion of Sapt-Sindhu lay in the pre-existing religious beliefs of Bavra world? Many more deities like Varuna, Nasataya etc. had come into existence. They were just not there in the pre-existing Baodh religion of Bavra people. Vedic religion got more enriched with these newly evolved deities. New mythological and philosophical explainations came up which further enriched this new religion. Initially, the religion of Aryans was no different from Bavra religion. We have seen how Zoroaster was often invited by Aryans for clearification of doubts. But it seems that, by the time of Rig-Veda, many significant new rites and rituals had evolved in the Aryan world.

These changes, apperantly, made the two religions so different from each other that Aryans started calling Non-Aryans i.e. Bavra people as 'Abrata' and 'Akratu'. 'Abrata' and 'Akratu' can be translated as – those who did not follow the holy rites and rituals that were prevalent among Aryans. Gradually, with the passage of time, this religion of Aryan world got transfigured to such an extent that it became a completely different religion. It was more evolved. It was, philosophically, more enriched and sound. People of nearby regions got attracted towards it. Even those, who had clung to the age-old Baodh philosophy, were getting fascinated by it. This was the era of gradual spread of Vedic philosophy. Most probably, these were the days when the following Avestan hymn was compiled –

Yatchit ushastaire Hindvo ageurvayeite,[1]
Yatchit daoshataire nighne.

In Khordeh Avesta – (Prayers in Roman Script and Translation in English written by Tehmurasp Rustamji Sethna) – this hymn is translated as –

Who reach Hindustan, which is in the Eastern direction,
and Niniveh, which is in the Western direction.

But I don't think this is the true meaning of this hymn. Firstly, 'Hindvo' can not be Hindustan. The word – Hindustan – is just not there in hymns of Gatha. 'Hindvo' conveys something plural. It exactly stands for – Hindus i.e. followers of Hindu religion. They were people inhabiting the Sapt-Sindhu religion, who had a distinct faith. This home land of Hindus was known to Avesta speaking ancient Iranians. In Avestan hymns, this home land of Vedic Aryans was called 'Haft-Hindvo'. Therefore, whenever they wanted to mention or talk about this land of Vedic Aryans, they referred to it as – 'Haft-Hindvo'. In this hymn, 'Hindvo' refers to a definite group of people, and not to some land.

Secondly, 'Nighne' can never be identified with some place called – Niniveh. It requires irrational stretch of imagination to equate 'nighne' with 'Niniveh'. 'Nighne' is identically found in Sanskrit as well. In Sanskrit, it means – disciple or follower. I know, it means exactly the same in this Avestan hymn too.

1 Khordeh Avesta – Sarosh Yasht Vadi – para – (29).

Similarly, 'Ushastaire' is identically found in both languages. It can never be – the Eastern direction. Here, the root word is – 'Ushas'. In Sanskrit, 'Ushas' stands for – dawn or day-break. In Avesta also, 'Usha' is dawn or the Goddess of Dawn. 'Ushastaire' exactly means – after dawn or when day breaks.

'Taire' is derived from the root word – 'tri'. It means – to spread. 'Ushastaire' is the early morning – when the dawn spreads or when the day breaks.

I don't know how 'daoshataire' can be explained as – the Western direction. It is identically found in Sanskrit as well. In Sanskrit, 'daoshataire' can be explained as – the time after sunset. Thus the true meaning of the aforesaid hymn is –

From early morning, where ever the Hindus move around,
(all those who come in contact) become their followers,
by the time darkness falls or the Sun sets.

The Avestan lines simply describe that the Hindus generally started their daily activities early in the morning. Through out the day, they kept wandering from one place to another. And all those, who came in their contact, became ardent followers of their religion. This process of adopting faith used to be generally complete by the end of the same day. Such was the eagerness of common men. Things are precisely clear. Initially, the religion of Aryans was no different from that of pre- existing Bavra world. But, with passage of time, things changed in Aryan world. New deities evolved. New rites and rituals came into existence. With these new modifications, the religion of Aryans became quite different from the age-old Bavra religion (Baodh). In Bavra world, this newly evolved religion of Aryans was given a new name. They called it Hindu religion. This nomenclature of religion of Vedic Aryans had nothing to do with Persians. We know that Avesta speaking earliest Zoroastrians were Indians. We know that most of the hymns of Gatha were compiled here – on Indian soil.

RAMA – NOT A MYTH

rAma XAstrvm Yazamaide[1]

This line can be observed many times in Gatha. In this Avestan line – 'A' is pronounced as 'a' in 'car' or 'far'. Avestan word 'rAma' of this hymn is explained in Zoroastrian texts as 'good' or 'good pasture'. The word 'XAstrvm' is explained as 'land' or 'kingdom' and 'Yazamaide' is, as usual, 'we worship hereby' or 'we revere hereby'. Thus, strictly according to their dictionary, the meaning of the aforesaid line becomes –

We revere, hereby, the good land (or kingdom).

Since each Avestan word of this hymn has almost exactly similar corresponding word in Vedic Sanskrit as well, let us observe what the aforesaid line would convey in Sanskrit. The corresponding similar word of Avestan 'XAstrvm' is Sanskrit 'kshatram' - which has exactly identical meaning. The Avestan 'yazamaide' is Vedic 'yazam ide'. It stands for - 'we worship hereby'. Therefore, in Vedic Sanskrit also, the meaning of 'XAstrvm Yazamaide' is exactly similar and it can be given as – 'we worship hereby the kingdom (or land)'. But we do not have any Sanskrit equivalent of 'rAma' with an identical meaning. 'Rama' in Sanskrit can only convey Lord Rama. In Vedic Sanskrit the line can be translated as –

We, hereby, worship the land (or kingdom) of Rama.

Besides 'good' or 'good pasture', Avestan 'rAma' has also been attributed many other meanings. At other places it is explained as – peace, happiness, joy. But isn't that strange? 'rAma' should not refer to such dissimilar things in Avesta and Vedic Sanskrit. Most of the Avestan words have corresponding

1 Gatha – yasna – 16 – para – (5).

similar words in Sanskrit. I think, here, some kind of error has certainly crept in. But there is no way out. The lead has to come again from Zoroastrian texts alone. There is an Avestan hymn of Gatha, which is also incorporated in Meher Niyaesh of Khordeh Avesta. It says –

rAm-shayanem hu-shayanem Airyabyo danghubyo[1]

Exactly according to Avestan explanation 'hu shayanem' is 'good shayanem'. 'hu' is the corresponding similar word of Sanskrit 'su'. These words convey exactly similar meaning. Avestan 'hu' or Sanskrit 'su' stands for – good, beautiful. If Avestan 'rAm' also stands for 'good' then the translation of 'rAm shayanem hu shayanem' will become – 'good shayanem is good shayanem'. This is absurd. It does not make sense – for any possible meaning that can be accorded to the word 'shayanem'. The true meaning of 'rAm' cannot be – good.

The meaning of the remaining words is clear and undisputed. 'Airyabyo' is 'of Aryans' and 'danghubyo' is 'country'. 'Airyabyo danghubyo' is translated as – country of Aryans. In religious books of Zoroastrians 'shayanem' is vaguely described as – dwelling. If we go exactly by Avestan translations, then the meaning of the hymn is –

Good dwelling is good dwelling in this country of Aryans

It doesn't make sense. We know that Avesta had become extinct thousands of years before. Its words were assigned specific meanings at much later stage. On the other hand the language Sanskrit still exists. Although modern Sanskrit is somewhat different from Vedic Sanskrit but more than ninety five percent of its words are identically found in ancient Vedic Sanskrit as well. These are the words that have lived through ages. They have not changed at all. They exist, even today, in same form, and with similar meaning. Avesta and

1 Khordeh Avesta – Meher Niyaesh – para – (13).

Sanskrit developed from the same stalk and all words, which are identically found in these languages, must be attributed to common origin. In both languages, these words must have been borrowed, from the common roots, in exactly similar form and with exactly similar meaning. 'shayanem' is one such word. It is identically found in both Avesta and Sanskrit. But, in Sanskrit, it still exists – in same form and with same meaning – as it existed thousands of years before, in Vedic era. Therefore we have reasons to believe what it meant initially. In Sanskrit – shayanem – conveys the meaning of governance, rule or administration. In Avasta also, initially, it must have conveyed the same sense. However, at some later stage, in Persia, a new meaning was assigned to this word. Avesta had become extinct and 'shayanem' was miss-explained as – dwelling. Therefore, we may reasonably come to conclusion what it meant when these hymns were compiled. 'shayanem' was definitely used there to describe – administration, rule or governance. Now, if we consider 'rAmno' to be the Avestan word for good, then the meaning of the line becomes –

Good governance is good governance in the country of Aryans.

Again it does not make any sense. 'rAm' cannot imply 'good' here. In fact it is the name of a person whose rule is being described. 'rAm shayanem' is 'the rule of Rama'. Now the whole thing makes a clear sense. It says – the rule of Lord Rama was the best rule in this country of Aryans. It refers to our concept of 'Rama-rajya'. That is exactly the way Lord Rama ruled in this country. It was the golden era of Aryan world. These Avestan lines become the earliest written record of the rule of Rama.

But religious stories are not always considered to have in their account details of historical truth. Hence, all historical truths that is available as an inseparable part of any sacred text, is also, quite often, set aside as mythological fictions. And the choice of common man, predictably, keeps taking sides between this dilemma of fact and fiction. It depends on their state of mind. Men with religious fervor consider sacred texts as nothing less than truth; men without it look for corroborative evidences from outside world. And the lack of any final opinion of general consensus keeps things in a hung state. Such confusions can only be settled by sudden appearance of some kind of evidence that either forcefully corroborates or rationally disproves the subject matter of any religious account. But the problem lies in the fact that the earliest written documents of almost all civilizations are of sacred nature. The very first hymns of Hindu religion are considered to be of divine origin. Vedas are believed to be heavenly revelation. Avesta literally means – 'revealed wisdom' and the earliest Zoroastrian texts were compiled in this sacred language. In Abrahmic religion, the first sacred text – Ten Commandments – was handed over to Moses by almighty. It was inscribed on stone slab. And 'Torah-Torah' literally means the Law of God that was given to Moses. It appears that, in the beginning, the art of writing was invented to describe divine communions alone. Hence, all written documents of earliest days of civilization are of religious nature. Can they be of any use in removing certain existing paradoxes? It is a big question.

I think the accounts available in different sacred texts can be intelligently employed to distinguish between truth and fiction. To illustrate, I will put forth an example from Babylonian mythology. Babylonian religious texts describe the construction of 'Tower of Babel'. This description alone would not have convinced many about the true existence of Tower of Babel. However, if similar account is found in the religious texts of Judaism as well, then the general opinion is going to be significantly affected. Observe the lines of the Book of Genesis –

'Let's build us a city and a tower whose top may reach unto heaven. -----Therefore is the name of it - called Babel.'

The followers of early Judaism were different people. Their mythology did not necessitate the existence of Tower of Babel. Yet it is there. It simply describes truth. It was the general description of physical world that existed in those days. Its mention in the Book of Genesis can be genuinely taken as true account of a historical monument. Though it is a different thing that the structural remains of this famous Tower of Babel is still existent but even if it were not available, this Biblical account was in itself, no weaker evidence to lead to the same conclusion

Similarly, the description of the kingdom of Rama and his golden rule in Avestan Gatha proves that Rama was a true historic figure. This more than five thousand years old treatise is not telling some story. It does not provide further details of the life of Rama. It does not grow into any mythological legend. It is just there. It certainly refers to the truth of surrounding world – an instance similar to the description of the Tower of Babel incorporated in the Book of Genesis. Both were facts. They were never required for building religious legends. Magnificent rule of Rama was a historical truth of that period. More than three thousand years were to lapse before Valmiki could compose the epic – Ramayana. Now, no one can say that Rama was a fictitious character designed by the poet Valmiki.

Valmiki composed the epic Ramayana some time in the later half of first millennium B.C. There are twenty-four thousand verses in it. It portrays each aspect of the life of Rama who was the crown prince of the kingdom of Ayodhya – a place situated in eastern part of the state of Uttar Pradesh in India. Long ago, king Dashrath ruled over the kingdom of Ayodhya. He had three wives – Kaushalya, Kaikayee and Sumitra. Kaushalya was the eldest. She was the mother of Rama. Kaikayee's son was Bharat whereas Sumitra had two sons – Lakshman and Shatrughna. Of all sons of Dashrath, Rama was the eldest and the ablest. He was declared the crown prince of Ayodhya. But just before his coronation Kaikayee managed that her own son – Bharat – would succeed king Dashrath. Besides, she also compelled king Dashrath to send Rama in exile for fourteen years. The old king, unwillingly, had to yield to her demands because he was bound to keep his promise. When Rama came to know about these developments, like an obedient son, he started preparations for exile. He was without any avarice. His wife – Sita – was a devoted and faithful lady. She also decided to go along with him. Even the perils and hardships of exile could not deter her decision. She just wanted to be with Rama – through all kinds of thick and thin. Even Lakshman – his younger brother – also took a similar decision. He had deep regards and love for his brother – Rama. He wanted to be with them so that he could substantially help them to overcome the adversities of jungle life. Rama, Sita and Lakshman bade farewell to their loved ones and proceeded into the forest that lay to the south of their kingdom. They were to spend fourteen long years in that jungle. Bharat was away while all these developments were taking place. When he came back to Ayodhya and was briefed about the state of affairs, he was shocked. Even he had deep regards for his eldest brother. He was bereft. He could not reconcile with decisions that were against the established norms. Rama, by virtue of being the eldest among them, was the rightful successor of king Dashrath. Bharat refused to become the king. He decided to act merely as a caretaker till the time Rama completed his exile and came back.

Rama, Sita and Lakshman kept roaming in dense forest that covered the entire central and southern peninsular region of India. The jungle was abode of many famous sages. It was general practice those days that people used to denounce all worldly pleasures and settle in forests practicing meditation. But the jungle was also the home of wild animals and dangerous demons. They often killed sages and devoured them. Thus, there existed perpetual threat to the lives of these holy men. When Rama saw all this, he came forward to their rescue. He was the bravest and ablest of all Aryans. To safeguard innocent men and sages, he killed many mighty demons and dragons. The sages felt safe and relieved. But Ravan – the demon king – came to know about their exile. He abducted Sita and went back to his kingdom that was in Sri Lanka. There ensued a war between Rama and Ravan. Ravan had a large and mighty army of demons. To counter that, Rama raised an army of apes and bears – who lived in that jungle and had developed great regards and liking for Rama. The battle of Rama and Ravan embodied the battle of good and evil. Finally, Rama killed Ravan. It was the victory of virtue over vice. He brought Sita back from captivity. When the period of exile was over, Rama, Sita and Lakshman came back to Ayodhya where Rama was coronated as king.

Each aspect of the life of Rama was portrayed in the epic Ramayana – extolling his virtues. Rama and his brothers were portrayed as ideals of the Aryan culture. This epic was believed to be the first written record of his life. But latter, with little variations, almost sixteen different stories came into existence. All these have been preserved in different ethnic groups of this world. And in each one of them – Rama and his brothers are always on the side of virtue. They are seen as obedient sons, brave warriors, loving husbands, ever ready to eradicate evil for the sake of goodness. Whether Valmiki conceived of a fictitious ideal character for his epic or the center stage character of Ramayana was a real person – till date, the opinion had been divided over this issue. A faction of people used to consider Rama as any other mythological divinity. On the other hand, there are millions in this world who believe in contrary. Although, in no way the glory of Rama is going to be affected adversely, even if he happened to be the literary work of a genius, yet we have reasons now, to believe of him as a real person. Almost five thousand years old Avestan texts corroborate the truth of Rama.

There is yet another line in Gatha that refers to Rama. It is believed that Ha-28 to Ha-53 is the work of Zoroaster himself. This is the part of Gatha that constitutes the oldest Avestan texts. Here, it is described that – for the safety of all good persons, lord Ahura gave Rama to the mankind.

wohu manamha YA huCvitis rAm&m ca data[1]

According to Avestan dictionary, the meaning of each word can be given as –

wohu manamha	–	good persons, sages
YA	–	whose
huCvitis	–	safety, safe dwelling
rAm&m	–	? (Lord Rama)
ca data	–	gave

Thus the whole line can be translated as – 'for the safety (or safe dwelling) of sages (you) gave Lord Rama'. We know that Rama had to spend fourteen long years in exile. During this period, he lived in forests that housed many wild animals and wicked demons. These forests were also the abode of many sages, who had, in their pursuit of knowledge, denounced world and settled deep inside jungle for meditation. Their life was severely endangered by these demons and wild beasts,

1 Gatha – Yasna – 29 – para (10).

which often killed and devoured them. Rama saw their plight and came forward to rescue them. Along with his younger brother, he fought and killed almost all demons. The sages felt relieved and lived safely and happily thereafter. Could it be that the earliest Zoroastrian people were aware of all this? Could it be that the mankind was indebted to Lord Rama and therefore Avesta speaking people chose to sincerely thank Lord Ahura for sending Rama to this world? I think that is exactly what these Avestan lines were designed to convey. You substitute the word 'rAm&m' with 'good' and the line becomes absurd. Safety or safe dwelling necessitates power, courage, bravery and valor, to be available for defense – in times of adversity. Rama was exactly that. He was the embodiment of virtue, courage and strength. 'rAm&m' exactly refers to Rama and is not 'good' or 'goodness' – as advocated.

Now observe the following hymn of Yasna – 65 of Gatha. It is also incorporated in Ardvi Sur Niyaesh of Khordeh Avesta.

Apo gatava ramoidhwem[1]
Yavata zaota yazaite

We are familiar with the story of Lord Rama. When Rama came to know that his wife 'Sita' was abducted by the demon king of Sri Lanka, he decided to attack his kingdom. He raised an army of monkeys and bear and marched towards Sri Lanka. But he got stuck at Rameshwaram, which was the tip of the landmass of Indian peninsula. There existed a vast ocean ahead. There was no land corridor between India and Sri Lanka through which an army could cross over. It was impossible, in those days, to tread such a huge stretch of water mass. Therefore, Rama began worshipping 'Apo' i.e. the Divine Waters to grant a safe passage. It is this significant incident of

1 Khordeh Avesta – Ardvi Sur Niyaesh – para – (9).

the life of Lord Rama that has been referred to in the hymn. 'Apo' is, as usual, 'the water' or 'the divinity that presides over waters of the world'. 'gatav' is derived from the root word 'ga' which refers to singing or chanting songs or hymns. 'ramo' can be translated as 'Lord Rama' and Avestan word 'idbum' is the corresponding identical of 'Idyum' of Sanskrit that can be translated as 'praise' or 'worship'. 'yavat' is both Avestan and Sanskrit word for 'whom'. 'zaota' can be translated as 'saints' or 'hermits' and 'yazaite' is understood in both languages as 'worship'. Thus, the whole passage can be translated as –

Even Lord Rama, whom the hermits worship,
sang hymns in praise of waters of the world.

And now we come to a very interesting hymn of Gatha. In Yasna – 49 of Zoroastrian Gatha, we come across the following hymn –

YaEC&m nOiT hwarStAiS W&s duZwarStA[1]

'YaEC&m' is corresponding identical of 'aesham' of Sanskrit. The capital 'C' of Avestan hymns is pronounced as 'sh'. In both languages the word stands for – this or like this. Its antonym in Avesta is 'anYaEC&m' which stands for – 'others' or 'different'. Avestan 'nOiT' is simply – 'not'. 'duZwarStA' is used on many occasions in Zoroastrian scriptures. There is no confusion about its meaning. 'duZwarStA' stands for – bad or immoral act. Thus, 'YaEC&m nOiT duZwarStA' can be translated exactly as – 'there is no bad or immoral act like this'. Now we come to the remaining part of the hymn. 'hwarStAiS W&s' must be referring to some kind of bad or immoral act. This act or deed has been declared as most abominable on earth and that no other immoral act is comparable with 'hwarStAiS W&s'. But these words, in their present form, do not convey any thing. Nothing can be conceived out of

1 Gatha – Yasna – 49 – para – (4).

'hwarStAiS W&s' that defines some kind of immoral or bad act. Could it be an erroneous transcription of some meaningful words? The capital 'W' of 'W&s' indicates that 'W' is the pre-dominant letter here which needs to be emphasized while pronouncing the word. 'sW' is the only word that can be erroneously transcribed as 'W&s'. 'sW' is both an Avestan as well as a Sanskrit word. It stands for – like or similar to. Thus the hymn can now be translated as –

There is no bad or immoral act that is similar to hwarStAiS.

This 'hwarStAiS' has to be a ghastly act which was known to ancient Zoroastrians. The intelligent use of capital letters makes it absolutely clear. It is erroneous transcription of – SitA harSw. SitA harSw is – abduction of Sita. It again, refers to the incidents related with Lord Rama. We know that Ravana, the Demon King, had abducted Sita. This act of Ravana was considered as – 'maha paap' or the meanest of all sins. Even in Ramayana, this act of Ravana is declared as most abominable and ghastly act of humanity. The Avestan hymn also declares the same. It says –

There is no bad or immoral act that is
comparable to abduction of Sita.

In Avestan texts Lord Rama is also mentioned as Raman Yazat. In Avestan scriptures 'Yazats' are deities. They are considered – worthy of worship. According to Zoroastrian mythology, to overcome a three headed demon, this Raman Yazat was invoked by Trit Atwya. It is also interesting to find that, according to the beautiful design of Mazdayasni theology, each month and each day of Zoroastrian religious calendar is presided over by a spiritual being. It is believed that the twenty-first day of each month is presided over by the Yazat called Rama.

But now we come to a very important aspect. If Avestan hymns were compiled on Iranian soil, then we will have to admit that ancient Zoroastrians must have been aware of all details of the golden era of Lord Rama. And not only that, they must have had knowledge of many more or all successive and previous rulers of India because, only then, they could compare, evaluate and finally pronounce their verdict that – the period of Rama was the golden era of Aryan world. How could that be? How could they be aware of each and every development that took place on Indian soil? However, let us presume that they had knowledge of every development that took place on Indian soil, but even then – 'rAmno kshatrahe yazamaide' appears distinctly out of context. Why natives of Persia would worship India? They worshipped the land of Rama because it was no different from their own. They worshipped this land because it was their home land. Observe what they have to say in Yasna 57 of Gatha –

dUrAt haca ahmAT nmAnAT[1]
dUrAT haca ahmAT WIsaT
dUrAT haca ahmAT zaNtaoT
dUrAT haca ahmAT dai?haot

'nmAnAT', 'WIsaT' and 'zaNtaoT' is home, village and town respectively. Similarly, 'dai?haot' is the erroneous transcription of – danghaot. Avestan 'danghaot' is explained as – country. The hymn says –

Far away is our home
Far away is our village
Far away is our town
Far away is our country

Most of the Avestan hymns were compiled in this country of Rama. Ancient Zoroastrians were definitely Indians.

1 Gatha – Yasna – 57 – para – (14).

It was at some later stage that they migrated to Persia, Babylon and to places further north and west. This early mass exodus of Aryans is clearly recorded even in religious books of Christianity. The Book of Genesis had come into existence any time before first millennium BC. Observe what it says –

'And it came to pass, as they journeyed from the east, they found a plain in the land of Shinai (Babylon), and they dwelt there.'

(Chapter 11)

It says – the kingdom of Babylon was founded by people who came from East. This again, is not part of any mythological legend. Yet it is there – recorded in the Book of Genesis. It simply describes the truth. To the east of Babylon lies only Iran and India. And we know that earliest Aryans who set foot on Iranian soil were people from India.

According to Sumerian mythology, the Gods came on to this earth from planate 'Nibiru'. On planate Nibiru, one year is called – a 'Sar' (isn't it corresponding identical of Indian 'sal'?). And one 'Sar' of Nibiru is equal to 3600 earth-years. They also believed that the total life span of 'Anunnaki' was 120 Sars. Thus they interpolated and fixed the total time-span of creation of world. They multiplied one hundred and twenty by three thousand six hundred – and derived the figure 432000 years. According to Sumerian mythology, the total life of this creation is 432000 years. Bewildering! In Vedic world too, one 'Kalyug' has exactly 432000years. It is true that different civilizations often get enriched by one another. Raman Yazat of Zoroastrian world was incorporated in Babylonian faith as well. Here Lord Rama became the Storm God. Even Babylonian mythology has an interesting legend. It says –

'The bird Zu endeavours to capture the tablets of fate from En- Lil, and during the contest which takes place in heaven, Zu seizes the tablet, which only Marduk can recover. Zu then goes into an inaccessible recess in the mountains, and Raman, the Storm God, is invoked to conquer him with his weapon – thunderbolt.'

The legend fairly gives out its eastern connection. Now observe the following line of Yasna 48 of Zoroastrian Gatha –

kOi drvgwOdvbIS xrUrAiS rAm&m dINtE[1]

'kOi' is, as usual, where, what, which. 'drvgwOdvbIS' is a verb which could be - waging war, attacking. It is derived from the root word – 'dru'. 'xrU' means demons. Here the root word is – 'kshah' or 'kshra'. In Sanskrit, 'kshapatah' means – Demon. 'Ramam' is Lord Rama and 'diNtE' stands for an act of giving. The hymn says –

'To wage war against all beastly demons, where else have you blessed mankind with some one like Lord Rama?'

This is not the only occasion where Rama is described attacking and terminating 'xrUrAiS' (Demons) of this world. There is yet another hymn on this subject. Observe what the following lines of Yasna (53) have to say –

huxCaqrAiS jVnvr&m xrUnvr&mcA[2]
rAm&mcA AiS dadAtU

'hu' exactly means good,pure, sacred, adorable etc. It is the corresponding identical of 'su' of Sanskrit. Avestan 'xCaqrA'(kshatra) is land, region, empire, place. Therefore, 'huxCaqrAiS' stands for – beautiful land or sacred empire. 'jVnvr&m' is the erroneous transcription of – 'Vnjvr&m'. The use of capital 'V' makes it absolutely clear. Here, the root word is 'Vnj' i.e. 'Vanj'. It is identically found in Sanskrit as well. 'Vanj' stands for – breaking, killing etc. In this hymn again, we

1 Gatha – Yasna – 48 – para – (11).
2 Gatha – Yasna – 53 – para – (8).

get the mention of – 'xrUnvr&m'. Here again, the root word 'xrU' is Demon. 'rAm&mcA Ais dadAtU' is simply – you gave to us Rama. The complete hymn can be translated as –

For killing of Demons in our sacred world
You gave to us – Lord Rama

And then, they proudly call their country as the abode of Lord Rama. The Avestan hymn says –

at hOi WAstrAi rAmA dI[1]

The meaning of each word of the hymn is as follows –

at – here
hOi – tobe, is
WAstrAi – place of residence, home
rAmA dI – of Lord Rama

The hymn attributes proper identity to the Avestan land. It says –

Here exists the place of residence of Lord Rama.

We know exactly where Lord Rama lived. His abode was not situated in Iran or Central Asia. This place of residence of Lord Rama was in India. Rama lived in the country from where the earliest Zoroastrians had emigrated. However, in those days, this country had a different name. It was Amavant. It was considered as the land of the rising Sun and hence, it was also called the land of Lord Ahura. Look what this hymn of Yasna 49 of Gatha has to say –

ArmatOiS kascIT aCA huzVNtuS[2]
tAiScA WispAiS qBahmI xCaqrOi ahurA

'kascIT' is the corresponding identical of Sanskrit word – 'Kashchit'. Even Avestan 'kascIT' is pronounced similarly.

1 Gatha – Yasna – 18 – para – (4).
2 Gatha – Yasna – 49 – para – (5).

It means - 'someone' or 'some body'. It always conveys an element of doubt. 'huzVNtuS' is the erroneous transcription of – huVzNtuS. 'Hu' is – good, beautiful. 'VzNtuS' can be translated as – worshipping, praying or chanting hymns in praise. Here, the root word is – Vaz (Vaj). It is identically found in Sanskrit as well. Even use of capital 'V' and 'N' makes it quite clear. The word 'Vajntus' is always pronounced laying emphasis on 'V' and 'N' only. We can not be wrong. We are not mistaken in suggesting that 'huzVNtuS' is the erroneous transcription of – 'hu VazNtuS'. In Yasna – 60, we again come across this word. Observe the hymn –

qBAw&s huzVNtuSv spvNtO mazdA[1]

'qBAw&s' is pronounced as – tbaw&s. It stands for – you all. 'spvNto' is pure, sacrosanct, sacred. Here the root word is – 'pav'. 'Mazda' is – bright rays of Lord Ahura. Thus, the whole line can be translated as –

You all should huzVNtuSv the bright rays
(given by Lord Ahura)

Here, 'huzVNtuSv' can not be any thing else. It is – hu VazNatuSv. It conveys an act of worship. It is – 'chanting beautiful hymns, in praise'.

But let us come back to the meaning of the hymn of Yasna – 49. The meaning of first line of the hymn becomes –

Where people sing beautiful hymns in
praise of some ArmatOiS

This 'ArmatOiS' has to be some divinity. Capital letters almost give it out. It is nothing but erroneously written – SitO-rAma. By the time this hymn was compiled, they had almost lost track of things. They did not know who SitO-rAma was. That is why they used the word 'kascIT' with SitO-rAma. But

1 Gatha – Yasna – 60 – para – (1).

they had heard about it. And they were told that the dwelling place of Lord Ahura was situated in the country of SitO-rAma. Observe what second line of the hymn has to say. The specific meaning of each word of the second line is as follows –

TAiScA – Their
WispAiS – World
QBhamI – Yours
xCaqrOi – area, empire, region
ahurA – Lord Ahura

It says – 'Your abode, Lord Ahura, lies in their country (or world).' The complete hymn can be translated as –

Where people sing beautiful hymns in praise of some SitO-rAma,
Your abode, Lord Ahura, lies in their country (or world).

This country was not Iran. The abode of Ahura lay in some other country of some other people. They knew – some SitO-rAma was worshipped there. Long back, it was left behind. They knew – it was situated far away.